Remembrance of God

A Selection of Bahá'í Prayers and Holy Writings

Bahá'í
PUBLISHING TRUST, INDIA

Seventh Edition: March 2001
Reprints: 2002, 2004, 2005, 2006, 2007, 2008
Revised Edition: 2012
2nd Revised Edition: March 2017

ISBN: 81-85091-64-1

Bahá'í Publishing Trust of India
F-3/6, Okhla Industrial Area, Phase I
New Delhi - 110020

Printed at :
Bosco Society for Printing & Graphic Training
Okhla Road, New Delhi - 110025
Ph.: 011-26910729 E-mail : boscopress@gmail.com

Blessed is the spot, and the house,
and the place, and the city,
and the heart, and the mountain,
and the refuge, and the cave,
and the valley, and the land,
and the sea, and the island,
and the meadow where mention
of God hath been made,
and His praise glorified.

—Bahá'u'lláh

Intone, O My servant, the verses of God that have been received by thee, as intoned by them who have drawn nigh unto Him, that the sweetness of thy melody may kindle thine own soul, and attract the hearts of all men. Whoso reciteth, in the privacy of his chamber, the verses revealed by God, the scattering angels of the Almighty shall scatter abroad the fragrance of the words uttered by his mouth, and shall cause the heart of every righteous man to throb. Though he may, at first, remain unaware of its effect, yet the virtue of the grace vouchsafed unto him must needs sooner or later exercise its influence upon his soul. Thus have the mysteries of the Revelation of God been decreed by virtue of the Will of Him Who is the Source of power and wisdom.

—BAHÁ'U'LLÁH

CONTENTS

Contents

Remembrance of God

Contents

Remembrance of God

Contents

PRAYERS
FOR SPECIAL OCCASIONS AND
HOLY WRITINGS

Contents

ASSISTANCE

O my God! I ask Thee, by Thy most glorious Name, to aid me in that which will cause the affairs of Thy servants to prosper, and Thy cities to flourish. Thou, indeed, hast power over all things!

—Bahá'u'lláh

* * *

O Thou Whose face is the object of my adoration, Whose beauty is my sanctuary, Whose habitation is my goal, Whose praise is my hope, Whose providence is my companion, Whose love is the cause of my being, Whose mention is my solace, Whose nearness is my desire, Whose presence is my dearest wish and highest aspiration, I entreat Thee not to withhold from me the things Thou didst ordain for the chosen ones among Thy servants. Supply me, then, with the good of this world and of the next.

Thou, truly, art the King of all men. There is no God but Thee, the Ever-Forgiving, the Most Generous.

—Bahá'u'lláh

Remembrance of God

Lauded be Thy name, O my God and the God of all things, my Glory and the Glory of all things, my Desire and the Desire of all things, my Strength and the Strength of all things, my King and the King of all things, my Possessor and the Possessor of all things, my Aim and the Aim of all things, my Mover and the Mover of all things! Suffer me not, I implore Thee, to be kept back from the ocean of Thy tender mercies, nor to be far removed from the shores of nearness to Thee.

Aught else except Thee, O my Lord, profiteth me not, and near access to anyone save Thyself availeth me nothing. I entreat Thee by the plenteousness of Thy riches, whereby Thou didst dispense with all else except Thyself, to number me with such as have set their faces towards Thee, and arisen to serve Thee.

Forgive, then, O my Lord, Thy servants and Thy handmaidens. Thou, truly, art the Ever-Forgiving, the Most Compassionate.

—Bahá'u'lláh

* * *

O Lord my God! Assist Thy loved ones to be firm in Thy Faith, to walk in Thy ways, to be steadfast in Thy Cause. Give them Thy grace to withstand the onslaught of self and passion, to follow the light of divine guidance. Thou art the Powerful, the Gracious, the Self-Subsisting, the Bestower, the Compassionate, the Almighty, the All-Bountiful.

—'Abdu'l-Bahá

* * *

Lord! Pitiful are we, grant us Thy favor; poor, bestow upon us a share from the ocean of Thy wealth; needy, do Thou satisfy us; abased, give us Thy glory. The fowls of the air and the beasts of the field receive their meat each day from Thee, and all beings partake of Thy care and loving-kindness.

Deprive not this feeble one of Thy wondrous grace and vouchsafe by Thy might unto this helpless soul Thy bounty.

Give us our daily bread, and grant Thine increase in the necessities of life, that we may be dependent on none other but Thee, may commune wholly with Thee, may walk in Thy ways and declare Thy mysteries. Thou art the Almighty and the Loving and the Provider of all mankind.

—'Abdu'l-Bahá

Remembrance of God

Remove not, O Lord, the festal board that hath been spread in Thy Name, and extinguish not the burning flame that hath been kindled by Thine unquenchable fire. Withhold not from flowing that living water of Thine that murmureth with the melody of Thy glory and Thy remembrance, and deprive not Thy servants from the fragrance of Thy sweet savors breathing forth the perfume of Thy love.

Lord! Turn the distressing cares of Thy holy ones into ease, their hardship into comfort, their abasement into glory, their sorrow into blissful joy, O Thou that holdest in Thy grasp the reins of all mankind!

Thou art, verily, the One, the Single, the Mighty, the All-Knowing, the All-Wise.

—'Abdu'l-Bahá

* * *

CHILDREN

O God, guide me, protect me, make of me a shining lamp and a brilliant star. Thou art the Mighty and the Powerful.

—'Abdu'l-Bahá

* * *

O God! Rear this little babe in the bosom of Thy love, and give it milk from the breast of Thy Providence. Cultivate this fresh plant in the rose garden of Thy love and aid it to grow through the showers of Thy bounty. Make it a child of the kingdom, and lead it to Thy heavenly realm. Thou art powerful and kind, and Thou art the Bestower, the Generous, the Lord of surpassing bounty.

—'Abdu'l-Bahá

* * *

O God! Educate these children. These children are the plants of Thine orchard, the flowers of Thy meadow, the roses of Thy garden. Let Thy rain fall upon them; let the Sun of Reality shine upon them with Thy love. Let Thy breeze refresh them in order that they may be trained, grow and develop, and appear in the utmost beauty. Thou art the Giver. Thou art the Compassionate.

—'Abdu'l-Bahá

* * *

O my Lord! O my Lord!
I am a child of tender years. Nourish me from the breast of Thy mercy, train me in the bosom of Thy love, educate me in the school of Thy guidance and develop me under the shadow of Thy bounty. Deliver me from darkness, make me a brilliant light; free me from unhappiness, make me a flower of the rose garden; suffer me to become a servant of Thy threshold and confer upon me the disposition and nature of the righteous; make me a cause of bounty to the human world, and crown my head with the diadem of eternal life.

Verily, Thou art the Powerful, the Mighty, the Seer, the Hearer.

—'Abdu'l-Bahá

Children

O Thou kind Lord! These lovely children are the handiwork of the fingers of Thy might and the wondrous signs of Thy greatness. O God! Protect these children, graciously assist them to be educated and enable them to render service to the world of humanity. O God! These children are pearls, cause them to be nurtured within the shell of Thy loving-kindness.

Thou art the Bountiful, the All-Loving.

—'Abdu'l-Bahá

* * *

O Lord! Make these children excellent plants. Let them grow and develop in the Garden of Thy Covenant, and bestow freshness and beauty through the outpourings from the clouds of the all-glorious Kingdom.

O Thou kind Lord! I am a little child, exalt me by admitting me to the kingdom. I am earthly, make me heavenly; I am of the world below, let me belong to the realm above; gloomy, suffer me to become radiant; material, make me spiritual, and grant that I may manifest Thine infinite bounties.

Thou art the Powerful, the All-Loving.

—'Abdu'l-Bahá

* * *

O God, my God! I supplicate confirmation and assistance for those who have arisen to serve Thy Cause and to educate the children who have been nurtured at the breast of Thy love. O God! Glorify these children in Thy kingdom and teach them from Thy knowledge. Thou art the Powerful and the Mighty.

—'Abdu'l-Bahá

* * *

CONTRIBUTIONS
TO THE FUND

O God, my God! Illumine the brows of Thy true lovers, and support them with angelic hosts of certain triumph. Set firm their feet on Thy straight path, and out of Thine ancient bounty open before them the portals of Thy blessings; for they are expending on Thy pathway what Thou hast bestowed upon them, safeguarding Thy Faith, putting their trust in their remembrance of Thee, offering up their hearts for love of Thee, and withholding not what they possess in adoration for Thy Beauty and in their search for ways to please Thee.

O my Lord! Ordain for them a plenteous share, a destined recompense and sure reward.

Verily, Thou art the Sustainer, the Helper, the Generous, the Bountiful, the Ever-Bestowing.

—'Abdu'l-Bahá

DEPARTED

This Prayer is to be used for Bahá'ís over the age of fifteen. It is the only Bahá'í obligatory prayer which is to be recited in congregation; it is to be recited by one believer while all present stand. There is no requirement to face the Qiblih when reciting this prayer.

* * *

O my God! This is Thy servant and the son of Thy servant who hath believed in Thee and in Thy signs, and set his face towards Thee, wholly detached from all except Thee. Thou art, verily, of those who show mercy the most merciful.

Deal with him, O Thou Who forgivest the sins of men and concealest their faults, as beseemeth the heaven of Thy bounty and the ocean of Thy grace. Grant him admission within the precincts of Thy transcendent mercy that was before the foundation of earth and heaven. There is no God but Thee, the Ever-Forgiving, the Most Generous. *Let him, then, repeat six times the greeting "Alláh-u-Abhá," and then repeat nineteen times each of the following verses:*

We all, verily, worship God.

We all, verily, bow down before God.

We all, verily, are devoted unto God.

We all, verily, give praise unto God.

We all, verily, yield thanks unto God.

We all, verily, are patient in God.

(If the dead be a woman, let him say: This is Thy handmaiden and the daughter of Thy handmaiden, etc. ...)

—Bahá'u'lláh

* * *

Glory be to Thee, O Lord my God! Abase not him whom Thou hast exalted through the power of Thine everlasting sovereignty, and remove not far from Thee him whom Thou hast caused to enter the tabernacle of Thine eternity.

Remembrance of God

Wilt Thou cast away, O my God, him whom Thou hast overshadowed with Thy Lordship, and wilt Thou turn away from Thee, O my Desire, him to whom Thou hast been a refuge? Canst Thou degrade him whom Thou hast uplifted, or forget him whom Thou didst enable to remember Thee?

Glorified, immensely glorified art Thou! Thou art He Who from everlasting hath been the King of the entire creation and its Prime Mover, and Thou wilt to everlasting remain the Lord of all created things and their Ordainer. Glorified art Thou, O my God! If Thou ceasest to be merciful unto Thy servants, who, then, will show mercy unto them; and if Thou refusest to succor Thy loved ones, who is there that can succor them?

Glorified, immeasurably glorified art Thou! Thou art adored in Thy truth, and Thee do we all, verily, worship; and Thou art manifest in Thy justice, and to Thee do we all, verily, bear witness. Thou art, in truth, beloved in Thy grace. No God is there but Thee, the Help in Peril, the Self-Subsisting.

—Bahá'u'lláh

* * *

Departed

O my God! O Thou forgiver of sins! Bestower of gifts! Dispeller of afflictions!

Verily, I beseech Thee to forgive the sins of such as have abandoned the physical garment and have ascended to the spiritual world.

O my Lord! Purify them from trespasses, dispel their sorrows, and change their darkness into light. Cause them to enter the garden of happiness, cleanse them with the most pure water, and grant them to behold Thy splendors on the loftiest mount.

—'Abdu'l-Bahá

* * *

DETACHMENT

Lauded be Thy name, O my God! I entreat Thee by the fragrances of the Raiment of Thy grace which at Thy bidding and in conformity with Thy desire were diffused throughout the entire creation, and by the Daystar of Thy will that hath shone brightly, through the power of Thy might and of Thy sovereignty, above the horizon of Thy mercy, to blot out from my heart all idle fancies and vain imaginings, that with all my affections I may turn unto Thee, O Thou Lord of all mankind!

I am Thy servant and the son of Thy servant, O my God! I have laid hold on the handle of Thy grace, and clung to the cord of Thy tender mercy. Ordain for me the good things that are with Thee, and nourish me from the Table Thou didst send down out of the clouds of Thy bounty and the heaven of Thy favor.

Thou, in very truth, art the Lord of the worlds, and the God of all that are in heaven and all that are on earth.

—Bahá'u'lláh

Detachment

Many a chilled heart, O my God, hath been set ablaze with the fire of Thy Cause, and many a slumberer hath been wakened by the sweetness of Thy voice. How many are the strangers who have sought shelter beneath the shadow of the tree of Thy oneness, and how numerous the thirsty ones who have panted after the fountain of Thy living waters in Thy days!

Blessed is he that hath set himself towards Thee, and hasted to attain the Dayspring of the lights of Thy face. Blessed is he who with all his affections hath turned to the Dawning-Place of Thy Revelation and the Fountainhead of Thine inspiration. Blessed is he that hath expended in Thy path what Thou didst bestow upon him through Thy bounty and favor. Blessed is he who, in his sore longing after Thee, hath cast away all else except Thyself. Blessed is he who hath enjoyed intimate communion with Thee, and rid himself of all attachment to anyone save Thee.

I beseech Thee, O my Lord, by Him Who is Thy Name, Who, through the power of Thy sovereignty and might, hath risen above the horizon of His prison, to ordain for everyone what becometh Thee and beseemeth Thine exaltation.

Thy might, in truth, is equal to all things.

—Bahá'u'lláh

* * *

Praise be unto Thee, O my God! I am one of Thy servants, who hath believed on Thee and on Thy signs. Thou seest how I have set myself towards the door of Thy mercy, and turned my face in the direction of Thy loving-kindness. I beseech Thee, by Thy most excellent titles and Thy most exalted attributes, to open to my face the portals of Thy bestowals. Aid me, then, to do that which is good, O Thou Who art the Possessor of all names and attributes!

I am poor, O my Lord, and Thou art the Rich. I have set my face towards Thee, and detached myself from all but Thee. Deprive me not, I implore Thee, of the breezes of Thy tender mercy, and withhold not from me what Thou didst ordain for the chosen among Thy servants.

Detachment

Remove the veil from mine eyes, O my Lord, that I may recognize what Thou hast desired for Thy creatures, and discover, in all the manifestations of Thy handiwork, the revelations of Thine almighty power. Enrapture my soul, O my Lord, with Thy most mighty signs, and draw me out of the depths of my corrupt and evil desires. Write down, then, for me the good of this world and of the world to come. Potent art Thou to do what pleaseth Thee. No God is there but Thee, the All-Glorious, Whose help is sought by all men.

I yield Thee thanks, O my Lord, that Thou hast wakened me from my sleep, and stirred me up, and created in me the desire to perceive what most of Thy servants have failed to apprehend. Make me able, therefore, O my Lord, to behold, for love of Thee and for the sake of Thy pleasure, whatsoever Thou hast desired. Thou art He to the power of Whose might and sovereignty all things testify.

There is none other God but Thee, the Almighty, the Beneficent.

—Bahá'u'lláh

* * *

Remembrance of God

O my God, my Lord and my Master! I have detached myself from my kindred and have sought through Thee to become independent of all that dwell on earth and ever ready to receive that which is praiseworthy in Thy sight. Bestow on me such good as will make me independent of aught else but Thee, and grant me an ampler share of Thy boundless favors. Verily, Thou art the Lord of grace abounding.

—The Báb

* * *

O Lord! Unto Thee I repair for refuge, and toward all Thy signs I set my heart.

O Lord! Whether traveling or at home, and in my occupation or in my work, I place my whole trust in Thee.

Grant me then Thy sufficing help so as to make me independent of all things, O Thou Who art unsurpassed in Thy mercy!

Bestow upon me my portion, O Lord, as Thou pleasest, and cause me to be satisfied with whatsoever Thou hast ordained for me.

Detachment

Thine is the absolute authority to command.

—The Báb

* * *

O God, my God! Thou art my Hope and my Beloved, my highest Aim and Desire! With great humbleness and entire devotion I pray to Thee to make me a minaret of Thy love in Thy land, a lamp of Thy knowledge among Thy creatures, and a banner of divine bounty in Thy dominion.

Number me with such of Thy servants as have detached themselves from everything but Thee, have sanctified themselves from the transitory things of this world, and have freed themselves from the promptings of the voicers of idle fancies.

Let my heart be dilated with joy through the spirit of confirmation from Thy kingdom, and brighten my eyes by beholding the hosts of divine assistance descending successively upon me from the kingdom of Thine omnipotent glory.

Thou art, in truth, the Almighty, the All-Glorious, the All-Powerful.

—'Abdu'l-Bahá

* * *

EXPECTANT MOTHERS

My Lord! My Lord! I praise Thee and I thank Thee for that whereby Thou hast favoured Thine humble maid-servant, Thy slave beseeching and supplicating Thee, because Thou hast verily guided her unto Thine obvious Kingdom and caused her to hear Thine exalted Call in the contingent world and to behold Thy Signs which prove the appearance of Thy victorious reign over all things.

O my Lord, I dedicate that which is in my womb unto Thee. Then cause it to be a praiseworthy child in Thy Kingdom and a fortunate one by Thy favor and Thy generosity; to develop and to grow up under the charge of Thine education. Verily, Thou art the Gracious! Verily, Thou art the Lord of Great Favor!

—'Abdu'l-Bahá

* * *

FAMILIES

Glory be unto Thee, O Lord my God! I beg Thee to forgive me and those who support Thy Faith. Verily, Thou art the sovereign Lord, the Forgiver, the Most Generous. O my God! Enable such servants of Thine as are deprived of knowledge to be admitted into Thy Cause; for once they learn of Thee, they bear witness to the truth of the Day of Judgment and do not dispute the revelations of Thy bounty. Send down upon them the tokens of Thy grace, and grant them, wherever they reside, a liberal share of that which Thou hast ordained for the pious among Thy servants. Thou art in truth the Supreme Ruler, the All-Bounteous, the Most Benevolent.

O my God! Let the outpourings of Thy bounty and blessings descend upon homes whose inmates have embraced Thy Faith, as a token of Thy grace and as a mark of loving-kindness from Thy presence. Verily, unsurpassed art Thou in granting forgiveness. Should Thy bounty be withheld from anyone, how could he be reckoned among the followers of the Faith in Thy Day?

Bless me, O my God, and those who will believe in Thy signs on the appointed Day, and such as cherish my love in their hearts—a love which Thou dost instill into them. Verily, Thou art the Lord of righteousness, the Most Exalted.

—The Báb

* * *

FIRMNESS IN THE COVENANT

He is the Mighty, the Pardoner, the Compassionate!

O God, my God! Thou beholdest Thy servants in the abyss of perdition and error; where is Thy light of divine guidance, O Thou the Desire of the world? Thou knowest their helplessness and their feebleness; where is Thy power, O Thou in Whose grasp lie the powers of heaven and earth?

I ask Thee, O Lord my God, by the splendor of the lights of Thy loving-kindness and the billows of the ocean of Thy knowledge and wisdom and by Thy Word wherewith Thou hast swayed the peoples of Thy dominion, to grant that I may be one of them that have observed Thy bidding in Thy Book. And do Thou ordain for me that which Thou hast ordained for Thy trusted ones, them that have quaffed the wine of divine inspiration from the chalice of Thy bounty and hastened to do Thy pleasure and observe Thy Covenant and Testament. Powerful art Thou to do as Thou willest. There is none other God but Thee, the All-Knowing, the All-Wise.

Decree for me, by Thy bounty, O Lord, that which shall prosper me in this world and hereafter and shall draw me nigh unto Thee, O Thou Who art the Lord of all men. There is none other God but Thee, the One, the Mighty, the Glorified.

—Bahá'u'lláh

* * *

O my Lord and my Hope! Help Thou Thy loved ones to be steadfast in Thy mighty Covenant, to remain faithful to Thy manifest Cause, and to carry out the commandments Thou didst set down for them in Thy Book of Splendors; that they may become banners of guidance and lamps of the Company above, wellsprings of Thine infinite wisdom, and stars that lead aright, as they shine down from the supernal sky.

Verily, art Thou the Invincible, the Almighty, the All-Powerful.

—'Abdu'l-Bahá

* * *

Make firm our steps, O Lord, in Thy path and strengthen Thou our hearts in Thine obedience. Turn our faces toward the beauty of Thy oneness, and gladden our bosoms with the signs of Thy divine unity. Adorn our bodies with the robe of Thy bounty, and remove from our eyes the veil of sinfulness, and give us the chalice of Thy grace; that the essence of all beings may sing Thy praise before the vision of Thy grandeur. Reveal then Thyself, O Lord, by Thy merciful utterance and the mystery of Thy divine being, that the holy ecstasy of prayer may fill our souls—a prayer that shall rise above words and letters and transcend the murmur of syllables and sounds—that all things may be merged into nothingness before the revelation of Thy splendor.

Lord! These are servants that have remained fast and firm in Thy Covenant and Thy Testament, that have held fast unto the cord of constancy in Thy Cause and clung unto the hem of the robe of Thy grandeur. Assist them, O Lord, with Thy grace, confirm with Thy power and strengthen their loins in obedience to Thee.

Thou art the Pardoner, the Gracious.

—'Abdu'l-Bahá

FORGIVENESS

I am he, O my Lord, that hath set his face towards Thee, and fixed his hope on the wonders of Thy grace and the revelations of Thy bounty. I pray Thee that Thou wilt not suffer me to turn away disappointed from the door of Thy mercy, nor abandon me to such of Thy creatures as have repudiated Thy Cause.

I am, O my God, Thy servant and the son of Thy servant. I have recognized Thy truth in Thy days, and have directed my steps towards the shores of Thy oneness, confessing Thy singleness, acknowledging Thy unity, and hoping for Thy forgiveness and pardon. Powerful art Thou to do what Thou willest; no God is there beside Thee, the All-Glorious, the Ever-Forgiving.

—Bahá'u'lláh

Forgiveness

Glorified art Thou, O Lord my God! I beseech Thee by Thy Chosen Ones, and by the Bearers of Thy Trust, and by Him Whom Thou hast ordained to be the Seal of Thy Prophets and of Thy Messengers, to let Thy remembrance be my companion, and Thy love my aim, and Thy face my goal, and Thy name my lamp, and Thy wish my desire, and Thy pleasure my delight.

I am a sinner, O my Lord, and Thou art the Ever-Forgiving. As soon as I recognized Thee, I hastened to attain the exalted court of Thy loving-kindness. Forgive me, O my Lord, my sins which have hindered me from walking in the ways of Thy good pleasure, and from attaining the shores of the ocean of Thy oneness.

There is no one, O my Lord, who can deal bountifully with me to whom I can turn my face, and none who can have compassion on me that I may crave his mercy. Cast me not out, I implore Thee, of the presence of Thy grace, neither do Thou withhold from me the outpourings of Thy generosity and bounty. Ordain for me, O my Lord, what Thou hast ordained for them that love Thee, and write down for me what Thou hast written down for Thy chosen ones. My gaze hath, at all times, been fixed on the horizon of Thy gracious providence, and mine eyes bent upon the court of Thy tender mercies. Do with me as beseemeth Thee. No God is there but Thee, the God of power, the God of glory, Whose help is implored by all men.

—Bahá'u'lláh

* * *

O God, my God! I implore Thee by the blood of Thy true lovers who were so enraptured by Thy sweet utterance that they hastened unto the Pinnacle of Glory, the site of the most glorious martyrdom, and I beseech Thee by the mysteries which lie enshrined in Thy knowledge and by the pearls that are treasured in the ocean of Thy bounty to grant forgiveness unto me and unto my father and my mother. Of those who show forth mercy, Thou art in truth the most Merciful. No God is there but Thee, the Ever-Forgiving, the All-Bountiful.

O Lord! Thou seest this essence of sinfulness turning unto the ocean of Thy favour and this

Forgiveness

feeble one seeking the kindom of Thy Divine
Power and this poor creature inclining himself
towards the day-star of thy wealth. By Thy mercy
and Thy grace, disappoint him not, O Lord, nor
debar him from the revelations of Thy bounty in
Thy days, nor cast him away from Thy door which
Thou hast opened wide to all that dwell in Thy
heaven and on Thine earth.

Alas! Alas! My sins have prevented me from
approaching the Court of Thy holiness and my
trespasses have caused me to stray far from the
Tabernacle of Thy majesty. I have committeed
that which Thou didst forbid me to do and have
put away what Thou didst ordain me to observe.

I pray Thee by Him Who is the sovereign
Lord of Names to write down for me with the
Pen of Thy bounty that which will enable me to
draw nigh unto Thee and will purge me from my
trespasses which have intervened between me and
Thy forgiveness and Thy pardon.

Verily, Thou art the Potent, the Bountiful. No
God is there but Thee, the Mighty, the Gracious.

—Bahá'u'lláh

Remembrance of God

Glorified art Thou, O Lord my God! Every time I venture to make mention of Thee, I am held back by my mighty sins and grievous trespasses against Thee, and find myself wholly deprived of Thy grace, and utterly powerless to celebrate Thy praise. My great confidence in Thy bounty, however, reviveth my hope in Thee, and my certitude that Thou wilt bountifully deal with me emboldeneth me to extol Thee, and to ask of Thee the things Thou dost possess.

I implore Thee, O my God, by Thy mercy that hath surpassed all created things, and to which all that are immersed beneath the oceans of Thy names bear witness, not to abandon me unto my self, for my heart is prone to evil. Guard me, then, within the stronghold of Thy protection and the shelter of Thy care. I am he, O my God, whose only wish is what Thou hast determined by the power of Thy might. All I have chosen for myself is to be assisted by Thy gracious appointments and the ruling of Thy will, and to be aided with the tokens of Thy decree and judgment.

I beseech Thee, O Thou Who art the Beloved of the hearts which long for Thee, by the

Forgiveness

Manifestations of Thy Cause and the Daysprings of Thine inspiration, and the Exponents of Thy majesty, and the Treasuries of Thy knowledge, not to suffer me to be deprived of Thy holy Habitation, Thy Fane and Thy Tabernacle. Aid me, O my Lord, to attain His hallowed court, and to circle round His person, and to stand humbly at His door.

Thou art He Whose power is from everlasting to everlasting. Nothing escapeth Thy knowledge. Thou art, verily, the God of power, the God of glory and wisdom.

Praised be God, the Lord of the worlds!

—Bahá'u'lláh

* * *

Praise be unto Thee, O Lord. Forgive us our sins, have mercy upon us and enable us to return unto Thee. Suffer us not to rely on aught else besides Thee, and vouchsafe unto us, through Thy bounty, that which Thou lovest and desirest and well beseemeth Thee. Exalt the station of them that have truly believed, and forgive them with Thy gracious forgiveness. Verily, Thou art the Help in Peril, the Self-Subsisting.

—The Báb

Remembrance of God

O Thou forgiving Lord! Thou art the shelter of all these Thy servants. Thou knowest the secrets and art aware of all things. We are all helpless, and Thou art the Mighty, the Omnipotent. We are all sinners, and Thou art the Forgiver of sins, the Merciful, the Compassionate. O Lord! Look not at our shortcomings. Deal with us according to Thy grace and bounty. Our shortcomings are many, but the ocean of Thy forgiveness is boundless. Our weakness is grievous, but the evidences of Thine aid and assistance are clear. Therefore, confirm and strengthen us. Enable us to do that which is worthy of Thy holy Threshold. Illumine our hearts, grant us discerning eyes and attentive ears. Resuscitate the dead and heal the sick. Bestow wealth upon the poor and give peace and security to the fearful. Accept us in Thy kingdom and illumine us with the light of guidance. Thou art the Powerful and the Omnipotent. Thou art the Generous. Thou art the Clement. Thou art the Kind.

—'Abdu'l-Bahá

***

GUIDANCE

My God, the Object of my adoration, the Goal of my desire, the All-Bountiful the Most Compassionate! All life is of Thee and all power lieth within the grasp of Thine omnipotence. Whosoever Thou exaltest is raised above the angels, and attaineth the station: "Verily, We uplifted him to a place on high!"; and whosoever Thou dost abase is made lower than dust, nay, less than nothing.

O Divine Providence! Though wicked, sinful, and intemperate, we still seek from Thee a "seat of truth," and long to behold the countenance of the Omnipotent King. It is Thine to command, and all sovereignty belongeth to Thee, and the realm of might boweth before Thy behest. Everything Thou doest is pure justice, nay, the very essence of grace. One gleam from the splendors of Thy Name, the All-Merciful, sufficeth to banish and blot out every trace of sinfulness from the world, and a single breath from the breezes of the Day of Thy Revelation is enough to adorn all mankind with a fresh attire.

Vouchsafe Thy strength, O Almighty One, unto Thy weak creatures, and quicken them who are as dead, that haply they may find Thee, and may be led unto the ocean of Thy guidance, and may remain steadfast in Thy Cause. Should the fragrance of Thy praise be shed abroad by any of the divers tongues of the world, out of the East or out of the West, it would, verily, be prized and greatly cherished. If such tongues, however, be deprived of that fragrance, they assuredly would be unworthy of any mention, be they words or thoughts.

We beg of Thee, O Providence, to show Thy way unto all men, and to guide them aright. Thou art, verily, the Almighty, the Most Powerful, the All-Knowing, the All-Seeing.

—Bahá'u'lláh

* * *

We pray to God to graciously assist them that have been led astray to be just and fair-minded, and to make them aware of that whereof they have been heedless. He, in truth, is the All-Bounteous, the Most Generous. Debar not Thy servants, O my Lord, from the door of Thy grace and drive them not away from the court of Thy presence. Assist them to dispel the mists of idle fancy, and to tear away the veils of vain imaginings and hopes. Thou art, verily, the All-Possessing, the Most High. No God is there but Thee, the Almighty, the Gracious.

—Bahá'u'lláh

* * *

Glorified art Thou, O Lord my God! Rain down, I beseech Thee, from the clouds of Thine overflowing grace, that which shall cleanse the hearts of Thy servants from whatever may prevent their beholding Thy face, or may prevent them from turning unto Thee, that they may all recognize Him Who is their Fashioner and Creator. Help them, then, O God, to reach forth, through the power of Thy sovereign might, towards such a station that they can readily distinguish every foul smell from the fragrance of the raiment of Him Who is the

Bearer of Thy most lofty and exalted name, that they may turn with all their affections toward Thee, and may enjoy such intimate communion with Thee that if all that is in heaven and on earth were given them they would regard it as unworthy of their notice, and would refuse to cease from remembering Thee and from extolling Thy virtues.

Shield, I pray Thee, O my Beloved, my heart's Desire, Thy servant who hath sought Thy face, from the darts of them that have denied Thee and from the shafts of such as have repudiated Thy Truth. Cause him, then, to be wholly devoted to Thee, to declare Thy Name, and to fix his gaze upon the sanctuary of Thy Revelation. Thou art, in truth, He who, at no time, hath turned away those who have set their hopes in Thee from the door of Thy mercy, nor prevented such as have sought Thee from attaining the court of Thy grace. No God is there but Thee, the Most Powerful the All-Highest, the Help in Peril, the All-Glorious, the All-Compelling, the Unconditioned.

—Bahá'u'lláh

Guidance

Say: O God, my God! Glory be to Thee for having guided me unto the horizon of Thy Revelation, illumined me with the splendors of the light of Thy grace and mercy, caused me to speak forth Thy praise, and given me to behold that which hath been revealed by Thy Pen.

I beseech Thee, O Thou the Lord of the kingdom of names and Fashioner of earth and heaven, by the rustling of the Divine Lote-Tree and by Thy most sweet utterance which hath enraptured the realities of all created things, to raise me up in Thy Name amidst Thy servants. I am he who hath sought in the daytime and in the night season to stand before the door of Thy bounty and to present himself before the throne of Thy justice. O Lord! Cast not away him who hath clung to the cord of Thy nearness, and deprive not him who hath directed his steps towards Thy most sublime station, the summit of glory, and the supreme objective— that station wherein every atom crieth out in the most eloquent tongue, saying: "Earth and heaven, glory and dominion are God's, the Almighty, the All-Glorious, the Most Bountiful!"

—Bahá'u'lláh

Remembrance of God

O God, my God! Give me to drink from the cup of Thy bestowal and illumine my face with the light of guidance. Make me firm in the path of faithfulness, assist me to be steadfast in Thy mighty Covenant, and suffer me to be numbered with Thy chosen servants. Unlock before my face the doors of abundance, grant me deliverance, and sustain me, through means I cannot reckon, from the treasuries of heaven. Suffer me to turn my face toward the countenance of Thy generosity and to be entirely devoted to Thee, O Thou Who art merciful and compassionate! To those that stand fast and firm in Thy Covenant Thou, verily, art gracious and generous. All praise be to God, the Lord of the worlds!

—'Abdu'l-Bahá

HANDMAIDENS

O Thou, at Whose dreadful majesty all things have trembled, in Whose grasp are the affairs of all men, towards Whose grace and mercy are set the faces of all Thy creatures! I entreat Thee, by Thy Name which Thou hast ordained to be the spirit of all names that are in the kingdom of names, to shield us from the whisperings of those who have turned away from Thee, and have repudiated the truth of Thy most august and most exalted Self, in this Revelation that hath caused the kingdom of Thy names to tremble.

I am one of Thy handmaidens, O my Lord! I have turned my face towards the sanctuary of Thy gracious favors and the adored tabernacle of Thy glory. Purify me of all that is not of Thee, and strengthen me to love Thee and to fulfill Thy pleasure, that I may delight myself in the contemplation of Thy beauty, and be rid of all attachment to any of Thy creatures, and may, at every moment, proclaim: "Magnified be God, the Lord of the worlds!"

Let my food, O my Lord, be Thy beauty, and my drink the light of Thy presence, and my hope Thy pleasure, and my work Thy praise, and my companion Thy remembrance, and my aid Thy sovereignty, and my dwelling-place Thy habitation, and my home the seat which Thou hast exalted above the limitations of them that are shut out as by a veil from Thee.

Thou art, in truth, the God of power, of strength and glory.

—Bahá'u'lláh

* * *

Glory be to Thee, O my God! My face hath been set towards Thy face, and my face is, verily, Thy face, and my call is Thy call, and my Revelation Thy Revelation, and my self Thy Self, and my Cause Thy Cause, and my behest Thy behest, and my Being Thy Being, and my sovereignty Thy sovereignty, and my glory Thy glory, and my power Thy power.

I implore Thee, O thou Fashioner of the nations and the King of eternity, to guard Thy handmaidens within the tabernacle of Thy chastity, and to cancel such of their deeds as are unworthy of Thy days. Purge out, then, from them, O my God, all doubts and idle fancies, and sanctify them from whatsoever becometh not their kinship with Thee, O Thou Who art the Lord of names, and the Source of utterance. Thou art He in Whose grasp are the reins of the entire creation.

No God is there but Thee, the Almighty, the Most Exalted, the All-Glorious, the Self-Subsisting.

—Bahá'u'lláh

* * *

O my Lord, my Beloved, my Desire! Befriend me in my loneliness and accompany me in my exile. Remove my sorrow. Cause me to be devoted to Thy beauty. Withdraw me from all else save Thee. Attract me through Thy fragrances of holiness. Cause me to be associated in Thy Kingdom with those who are severed from all else save Thee, who long to serve Thy sacred threshold and who stand to work in Thy Cause. Enable me to be one of Thy maidservants who have attained to Thy good pleasure. Verily, Thou art the Gracious, the Generous.

—'Abdu'l-Bahá

OThou most glorious Lord! Make this little maidservant of Thine blessed and happy; cause her to be cherished at the threshold of Thy oneness and let her drink deep from the cup of Thy love so that she may be filled with rapture and ecstasy and diffuse sweet-scented fragrance. Thou art the Mighty and the Powerful, and Thou art the All-Knowing, the All-Seeing.

—'Abdu'l-Bahá

* * *

OThou kind Lord! Bestow heavenly confirmation upon this daughter of the Kingdom and graciously aid her that she may remain firm and steadfast in Thy Cause and that she may, even as a nightingale of the rose garden of mysteries, warble melodies in the Abhá Kingdom in most wondrous tones, thereby bringing happiness to everyone. Make her exalted among the daughters of the Kingdom and enable her to attain life eternal.

Thou art the Bestower, the All-Loving.

—'Abdu'l-Bahá

HEALING

O God, my God! I beg of Thee by the ocean of Thy healing, and by the splendors of the Daystar of Thy grace, and by Thy Name through which Thou didst subdue Thy servants, and by the pervasive power of Thy most exalted Word and the potency of Thy most august Pen, and by Thy mercy that hath preceded the creation of all who are in heaven and on earth, to purge me with the waters of Thy bounty from every affliction and disorder, and from all weakness and feebleness.

Thou seest, O my Lord, Thy suppliant waiting at the door of Thy bounty, and him who hath set his hopes on Thee clinging to the cord of Thy generosity. Deny him not, I beseech Thee, the things he seeketh from the ocean of Thy grace and the Daystar of Thy loving-kindness.

Powerful art Thou to do what pleaseth Thee. There is none other God save Thee, the Ever-Forgiving, the Most Generous. —Bahá'u'lláh

Remembrance of God

Thy name is my healing, O my God, and remembrance of Thee is my remedy. Nearness to Thee is my hope, and love for Thee is my companion. Thy mercy to me is my healing and my succor in both this world and the world to come. Thou, verily, art the All-Bountiful, the All-Knowing, the All-Wise.

—Bahá'u'lláh

* * *

Glory be to Thee, O Lord my God! I beg of Thee by Thy Name through which He Who is Thy Beauty hath been stablished upon the throne of Thy Cause, and by Thy Name through which Thou changest all things, and gatherest together all things, and callest to account all things, and rewardest all things, and preservest all things, and sustainest all things—I beg of Thee to guard this handmaiden who hath fled for refuge to Thee, and hath sought the shelter of Him in Whom Thou Thyself art manifest, and hath put her whole trust and confidence in Thee.

She is sick, O my God, and hath entered beneath the shadow of the Tree of Thy healing;

afflicted, and hath fled to the City of Thy protection; diseased, and hath sought the Fountainhead of Thy favors; sorely vexed, and hath hasted to attain the Wellspring of Thy tranquillity; burdened with sin, and hath set her face toward the court of Thy forgiveness.

Attire her, by Thy sovereignty and Thy loving-kindness, O my God and my Beloved, with the raiment of Thy balm and Thy healing, and make her quaff of the cup of Thy mercy and Thy favors. Protect her, moreover, from every affliction and ailment, from all pain and sickness, and from whatsoever may be abhorrent unto Thee.

Thou, in truth, art immensely exalted above all else except Thyself. Thou art, verily, the Healer, the All-Sufficing, the Preserver, the Ever-Forgiving, the Most Merciful.

—Bahá'u'lláh

* * *

Thou art He, O my God, through Whose names the sick are healed and the ailing are restored, and the thirsty are given drink, and the sore-vexed are transquilized, and the wayward are guided, and the abased are exalted, and the poor are enriched, and the ignorant are enlightened, and the gloomy are illumined, and the sorrowful are cheered, and the chilled are warmed, and the downtrodden are raised up. Through Thy name, O my God, all created things were stirred up, and the heavens were spread and the earth was established and the clouds were raised and made to rain upon the earth. This, verily, is a token of Thy grace unto all Thy creatures.

I implore Thee, therefore, by Thy name through which Thou didst manifest Thy Godhead, and didst exalt Thy Cause above all creation, and by each of Thy most excellent titles and most august attributes, and by all the virtues wherewith Thy transcendent and most exalted Being is extolled, to send down this night from the clouds of Thy mercy the rains of Thy healing upon this suckling, whom Thou hast related unto Thine all-glorious Self in the kingdom of Thy creation. Clothe him, then, O my God, by Thy grace, with the robe of well-being and health, and guard him, O my Beloved, from every affliction and disorder, and from whatsoever is obnoxious unto Thee. Thy might, verily, is equal to all things. Thou, in truth, art the Most Powerful, the Self-Subsisting. Send down, moreover, upon him, O my God, the good of this world and of the next, and the good of the former and latter generations. Thy might and Thy wisdom are, verily, equal unto this.

—Bahá'u'lláh

* * *

Glory be to Thee, O Lord my God! I implore Thee by Thy Name, through which Thou didst lift up the ensigns of Thy guidance, and didst shed the radiance of Thy loving-kindness, and didst reveal the sovereignty of Thy Lordship; through which the lamp of Thy names hath appeared within the niche of Thine attributes, and He Who is the Tabernacle of Thy unity and the Manifestation of detachment hath shone forth; through which the ways of Thy guidance were made known, and the paths of Thy good pleasure were marked out; through which the foundations of error have been made to tremble, and the signs of wickedness have been abolished; through which the fountains of wisdom have burst forth, and the heavenly table hath been sent down; through which Thou didst preserve Thy servants and didst vouchsafe Thy healing; through which Thou didst show forth Thy tender mercies unto Thy servants and revealedst Thy forgiveness amidst Thy creatures—I implore Thee to keep safe him who hath held fast and returned unto Thee, and clung to Thy mercy, and seized the hem of Thy loving providence. Send down, then, upon him Thy healing, and make him whole, and endue him with a constancy vouchsafed by Thee, and a tranquillity bestowed by Thy highness.

Thou art, verily, the Healer, the Preserver, the Helper, the Almighty, the Powerful, the All-Glorious, the All-Knowing.

—Bahá'u'lláh

HUSBANDS

O God, my God! This Thy handmaid is calling upon Thee, trusting in Thee, turning her face unto Thee, imploring Thee to shed Thy heavenly bounties upon her, and to disclose unto her Thy spiritual mysteries, and to cast upon her the lights of Thy Godhead.

O my Lord! Make the eyes of my husband to see. Rejoice Thou his heart with the light of the knowledge of Thee, draw Thou his mind unto Thy luminous beauty, cheer Thou his spirit by revealing unto him Thy manifest splendors.

O my Lord! Lift Thou the veil from before his sight. Rain down Thy plenteous bounties upon him, intoxicate him with the wine of love for Thee, make him one of Thy angels whose feet walk upon this earth even as their souls are soaring through the high heavens. Cause him to become a brilliant lamp, shining out with the light of Thy wisdom in the midst of Thy people.

Verily, Thou art the Precious, the Ever-Bestowing, the Open of Hand.

—'Abdu'l-Bahá

* * *

JOURNEY

O God, my God! I have set out from my home, holding fast unto the cord of Thy love, and I have committed myself wholly to Thy care and Thy protection. I entreat Thee by Thy power through which Thou didst protect Thy loved ones from the wayward and the perverse, and from every contumacious oppressor, and every wicked doer who hath strayed far from Thee, to keep me safe by Thy bounty and Thy grace. Enable me, then, to return to my home by Thy power and Thy might. Thou art, truly, the Almighty, the Help in Peril, the Self-Subsisting.

—Bahá'u'lláh

* * *

I have risen this morning by Thy grace, O my God, and left my home trusting wholly in Thee, and committing myself to Thy care. Send down, then, upon me, out of the heaven of Thy mercy, a blessing from Thy side, and enable me to return home in safety even as Thou didst enable me to set out under Thy protection with my thoughts fixed steadfastly upon Thee.

There is none other God but Thee, the One, the Incomparable, the All-Knowing, the All-Wise.

—Bahá'u'lláh

***

JUSTICE

SAY: O God, my God! Attire mine head with the crown of justice, and my temple with the ornament of equity. Thou, verily, art the Possessor of all gifts and bounties.

— Bahá'u'lláh

* * *

MANKIND

My God, Whom I worship and adore! I bear witness unto Thy unity and Thy oneness, and acknowledge Thy gifts, both in the past and in the present. Thou art the All-Bountiful, the overflowing showers of Whose mercy have rained down upon high and low alike, and the splendors of Whose grace have been shed over both the obedient and the rebellious.

O God of mercy, before Whose door the quintessence of mercy hath bowed down, and round the sanctuary of Whose Cause loving-kindness, in its inmost spirit, hath circled, we beseech Thee, entreating Thine ancient grace, and seeking Thy present favor, that Thou mayest have mercy upon all who are the manifestations of the world of being, and deny them not the outpourings of Thy grace in Thy days.

All are but poor and needy, and Thou, verily, art the All-Possessing, the All-Subduing, the All-Powerful.

—Bahá'u'lláh

Mankind

O Thou compassionate Lord, Thou Who art generous and able! We are servants of Thine sheltered beneath Thy providence. Cast Thy glance of favor upon us. Give light to our eyes, hearing to our ears, and understanding and love to our hearts. Render our souls joyous and happy through Thy glad tidings. O Lord! Point out to us the pathway of Thy kingdom and resuscitate all of us through the breaths of the Holy Spirit. Bestow upon us life everlasting and confer upon us never-ending honor. Unify mankind and illumine the world of humanity. May we all follow Thy pathway, long for Thy good pleasure and seek the mysteries of Thy kingdom. O God! Unite us and connect our hearts with Thy indissoluble bond. Verily, Thou art the Giver, Thou art the Kind One and Thou art the Almighty.

—'Abdu'l-Bahá

* * *

O Thou kind Lord! Thou hast created all humanity from the same stock. Thou hast decreed that all shall belong to the same household. In Thy Holy Presence they are all Thy servants, and all mankind are sheltered beneath Thy Tabernacle; all have gathered together at Thy Table of Bounty; all are illumined through the light of Thy Providence.

O God! Thou art kind to all, Thou hast provided for all, dost shelter all, conferrest life upon all. Thou hast endowed each and all with talents and faculties, and all are submerged in the Ocean of Thy Mercy.

O Thou kind Lord! Unite all. Let the religions agree and make the nations one, so that they may see each other as one family and the whole earth as one home. May they all live together in perfect harmony.

O God! Raise aloft the banner of the oneness of mankind.

O God! Establish the Most Great Peace.

Cement Thou, O God, the hearts together.

O Thou kind Father, God! Gladden our hearts through the fragrance of Thy love. Brighten our eyes through the Light of Thy Guidance. Delight our ears with the melody of Thy Word, and shelter us all in the Stronghold of Thy Providence.

Thou art the Mighty and Powerful, Thou art the Forgiving and Thou art the One Who overlooketh the shortcomings of all mankind.

—'Abdu'l-Bahá

Mankind

O God! we are weak; give us strength. We are poor; bestow upon us Thine illimitable treasures. We are sick; grant us Thy divine healing. We are powerless; give us of Thy heavenly power. O Lord! make us useful in this world; free us from the condition of self and desire. O Lord! make us firm in Thy love and cause us to be loving toward the whole of mankind. Confirm us in service to the world of humanity, so that we may become the servants of Thy servants, that we may love all Thy creatures and become compassionate to all Thy people. O Lord! Thou art the Almighty! Thou art the Merciful! Thou art the Forgiver! Thou art the Omnipotent.

—'Abdu'l-Bahá

MEETINGS

O Thou compassionate, Almighty One! This assemblage of souls have turned their faces unto Thee in supplication. With the utmost humility and submission they look toward Thy Kingdom and beg Thee for pardon and forgiveness. O God! endear this assembly to Thyself. Sanctify these souls and cast upon them the rays of Thy guidance. Illumine their hearts and gladden their spirits with Thy glad tidings. Receive all of them in Thy holy Kingdom, confer upon them Thine inexhaustible bounty, make them happy in this world and in the world to come.

—'Abdu'l-Bahá

* * *

O God! Verily we have gathered here in the fragrance of Thy love. We have turned to Thy Kingdom. We seek naught save Thee and desire nothing save Thy good-pleasure. O God! Let this food be Thy manna from heaven and grant this assemblage may be a concourse of Thy supreme ones. May they be the quickening cause of love to humanity and the source of illumination to the human race. May they be the instruments of Thy guidance upon earth. Verily, Thou art Powerful, Thou art the Bestower, Thou art the Forgiver, and Thou art the Almighty!

—'Abdu'l-Bahá

* * *

ODivine Providence! This assemblage is composed of Thy friends who are attracted to Thy beauty and are set ablaze by the fire of Thy love. Turn these souls into heavenly angels, resuscitate them through the breath of Thy Holy Spirit, grant them eloquent tongues and resolute hearts, bestow upon them heavenly power and merciful susceptibilities, cause them to become the promulgators of the oneness of mankind and the cause of love and concord in the world of humanity, so that the perilous darkness of ignorant prejudice may vanish through the light of the Sun of Truth, this dreary world may become illumined, this material realm may absorb the rays of the world of spirit, these different colors may merge into one color and the melody of praise may rise to the kingdom of Thy sanctity.

Verily, Thou art the Omnipotent, and the Almighty!

—'Abdu'l-Bahá

* * *

O my God! O my God! Verily, these servants are turning to Thee, supplicating Thy kingdom of mercy. Verily, they are attracted by Thy holiness and set aglow with the fire of Thy love, seeking confirmation from Thy wondrous kingdom, and hoping for attainment in Thy heavenly realm. Verily, they long for the descent of Thy bestowal, desiring illumination from the Sun of Reality. O Lord! Make them radiant lamps, merciful signs, fruitful trees and shining stars. May they come forth in Thy service and be connected with Thee by the bonds and ties of Thy love, longing for the lights of Thy favor. O Lord! Make them signs of guidance, standards of Thine immortal kingdom, waves of the sea of Thy mercy, mirrors of the light of Thy majesty.

Verily, Thou art the Generous. Verily, Thou art the Merciful. Verily, Thou art the Precious, the Beloved.

—'Abdu'l-Bahá

* * *

He is God!

O God, my God! I beseech Thee with a heart throbbing with Thy love, and I call upon Thee in the dark of the night, saying: O God! Aid me by Thy grace and mercy, and cause me to utter Thy praise amidst Thy creatures. O God, my God! These are Thy servants who have turned towards the right hand of Thy bounty, who have gathered together and been attracted to Thy call, and who have confessed Thy oneness. O Lord! Cause them to be signs of Thy mercy amongst Thy people and the banners of Thy bounty amidst Thy servants. O Lord! Send down upon them Thy blessings, illumine their hearts with the light of Thy knowledge, gladden their bosoms with the signs of Thy transcendent holiness, and make them as lamps shining with the light of Thy love. Thou, verily, art the Bountiful, the Compassionate.

Remembrance of God

O Lord, my Lord! This is a city wherein have gathered the exalted and prominent ones of the land. Guide them to Thy straight path and solace their eyes with Thy resplendent light. Suffer them to become servants to the cause of the oneness of humanity, standard-bearers of Thy most great bounty betwixt earth and heaven, strivers for peace and amity, and seekers of imperishable glory for all peoples. Verily, Thou art the Bountiful. Verily, Thou art the Compassionate. Verily, Thou art the Almighty.

—'Abdu'l-Bahá

MORNING

I have wakened in Thy shelter, O my God, and it becometh him that seeketh that shelter to abide within the Sanctuary of Thy protection and the Stronghold of Thy defense. Illumine my inner being, O my Lord, with the splendors of the Dayspring of Thy Revelation, even as Thou didst illumine my outer being with the morning light of Thy favor.

—Bahá'u'lláh

* * *

O my God and my Master! I am Thy servant and the son of Thy servant. I have risen from my couch at this dawntide when the Daystar of Thy oneness hath shone forth from the Dayspring of Thy will, and hath shed its radiance upon the whole world, according to what had been ordained in the Books of Thy Decree.

Praise be unto Thee, O my God, that we have wakened to the splendors of the light of Thy knowledge. Send down, then, upon us, O my Lord, what will enable us to dispense with anyone but Thee, and will rid us of all attachment to aught except Thyself. Write down, moreover, for me, and for such as are dear to me, and for my kindred, man and woman alike, the good of this world and the world to come. Keep us safe, then, through Thine unfailing protection, O Thou the Beloved of the entire creation and the Desire of the whole universe, from them whom Thou hast made to be the manifestations of the Evil Whisperer, who whisper in men's breasts. Potent art Thou to do Thy pleasure. Thou art, verily, the Almighty, the Help in Peril, the Self-Subsisting.

Bless Thou, O Lord my God, Him Whom Thou hast set over Thy most excellent Titles, and through Whom Thou hast divided between the godly and the wicked, and graciously aid us to do what Thou lovest and desirest. Bless Thou, moreover, O my God, them Who are Thy Words and Thy Letters, and them who have set their faces towards Thee, and turned unto Thy face, and hearkened to Thy Call.

Thou art, truly, the Lord and King of all men, and art potent over all things.

—Bahá'u'lláh

Morning

I give praise to Thee, O my God, that Thou hast awakened me out of my sleep, and brought me forth after my disappearance, and raised me up from my slumber. I have wakened this morning with my face set toward the splendors of the Daystar of Thy Revelation, through Which the heavens of Thy power and Thy majesty have been illumined, acknowledging Thy signs, believing in Thy Book, and holding fast unto Thy Cord.

I beseech Thee, by the potency of Thy will and the compelling power of Thy purpose, to make of what Thou didst reveal unto me in my sleep the surest foundation for the mansions of Thy love that are within the hearts of Thy loved ones, and the best instrument for the revelation of the tokens of Thy grace and Thy loving-kindness.

Do Thou ordain for me through Thy most exalted Pen, O my Lord, the good of this world and of the next. I testify that within Thy grasp are held the reins of all things. Thou changest them as Thou pleasest. No God is there save Thee, the Strong, the Faithful.

Remembrance of God

Thou art He Who changeth through His bidding abasement into glory, and weakness into strength, and powerlessness into might, and fear into calm, and doubt into certainty. No God is there but Thee, the Mighty, the Beneficent.

Thou disappointest no one who hath sought Thee, nor dost Thou keep back from Thee anyone who hath desired Thee. Ordain Thou for me what becometh the heaven of Thy generosity, and the ocean of Thy bounty. Thou art, verily, the Almighty, the Most Powerful.

—Bahá'u'lláh

***

NIGHT

How can I choose to sleep, O God, my God, when the eyes of them that long for Thee are wakeful because of their separation from Thee; and how can I lie down to rest whilst the souls of Thy lovers are sore vexed in their remoteness from Thy presence?

I have committed, O my Lord, my spirit and my entire being into the right hand of Thy might and Thy protection, and I lay my head on my pillow through Thy power, and lift it up according to Thy will and Thy good pleasure. Thou art, in truth, the Preserver, the Keeper, the Almighty, the Most Powerful.

By Thy might! I ask not, whether sleeping or waking, but that which Thou dost desire. I am Thy servant and in Thy hands. Do Thou graciously aid me to do what will shed forth the fragrance of Thy good pleasure. This, truly, is my hope and the hope of them that enjoy near access to Thee. Praised be Thou, O Lord of the worlds!

—Bahá'u'lláh

Remembrance of God

O my God, my Master, the Goal of my desire! This, Thy servant, seeketh to sleep in the shelter of Thy mercy, and to repose beneath the canopy of Thy grace, imploring Thy care and Thy protection.

I beg of Thee, O my Lord, by Thine eye that sleepeth not, to guard mine eyes from beholding aught beside Thee. Strengthen, then, their vision that they may discern Thy signs, and behold the Horizon of Thy Revelation. Thou art He before the revelations of Whose omnipotence the quintessence of power hath trembled.

No God is there but Thee, the Almighty, the All-Subduing, the Unconditioned.

—Bahá'u'lláh

* * *

"O seeker of Truth! If thou desirest that God may open thine eye, thou must supplicate unto God, pray to and commune with Him at midnight, saying:"

O Lord, I have turned my face unto Thy kingdom of oneness and am immersed in the sea of Thy mercy. O Lord, enlighten my sight by beholding Thy lights in this dark night, and make me happy by the wine of Thy love in this wonderful age. O Lord, make me hear Thy call, and open before my face the doors of Thy heaven, so that I may see the light of Thy glory and become attracted to Thy beauty.

Verily, Thou art the Giver, the Generous, the Merciful, the Forgiving.

—'Abdu'l-Bahá

***

PARENTS

Thou seest, O Lord, our suppliant hands lifted up towards the heaven of Thy favour and bounty. Grant that they may be filled with the treasures of Thy munificence and bountiful favors. Forgive us, and our fathers and our mothers, and fulfill whatsoever we have desired from the ocean of Thy grace and Divine generosity. Accept, O Beloved of our hearts all our works in Thy path. Thou art, verily, the Most Powerful, the Most Exalted, the Incomparable, the One, the Forgiving, the Gracious.

—Bahá'u'lláh

* * *

I beg Thy forgiveness, O my God, and implore pardon after the manner Thou wishest Thy servants to direct themselves to Thee. I beg of Thee to wash away our sins as befitteth Thy Lordship, and to forgive me, my parents, and those who in Thy estimation have entered the abode of Thy love in a manner which is worthy of Thy transcendent sovereignty and well beseemeth the glory of Thy celestial power.

O my God! Thou hast inspired my soul to offer its supplication to Thee, and but for Thee, I would not call upon Thee. Lauded and glorified art Thou; I yield Thee praise inasmuch as Thou didst reveal Thyself unto me, and I beg Thee to forgive me, since I have fallen short in my duty to know Thee and have failed to walk in the path of Thy love.

—The Báb

* * *

O Lord! In this Most Great Dispensation Thou dost accept the intercession of children in behalf of their parents. This is one of the special infinite bestowals of this Dispensation. Therefore, O Thou kind Lord, accept the request of this Thy servant at the threshold of Thy singleness and submerge his father in the ocean of Thy grace, because this son hath arisen to render Thee service and is exerting effort at all times in the pathway of Thy love. Verily, Thou art the Giver, the Forgiver and the Kind!

—'Abdu'l-Bahá

PIONEERS

Thou knowest, O God, and art my witness, that I have no desire in my heart save to attain Thy good pleasure, to be confirmed in servitude unto Thee, to consecrate myself in Thy service, to labor in Thy great vineyard and to sacrifice all in Thy path. Thou art the All-Knowing and the All-Seeing. I have no wish save to turn my steps, in my love for Thee, towards the mountains and the deserts, to loudly proclaim the advent of Thy Kingdom, and to raise Thy call amidst all men. O God! Open Thou the way for this helpless one, grant Thou the remedy to this ailing one and bestow Thy healing upon this afflicted one. With burning heart and tearful eyes I supplicate Thee at Thy Threshold.

O God! I am prepared to endure any ordeal in Thy path and desire with all my heart and soul to meet any hardship.

Pioneers

O God! Protect me from tests. Thou knowest full well that I have turned away from all things and freed myself of all thoughts. I have no occupation save mention of Thee and no aspiration save serving Thee.

—'Abdu'l-Bahá

* * *

PRAISE AND GRATITUDE

All praise, O my God, be to Thee Who art the Source of all glory and majesty, of greatness and honor, of sovereignty and dominion, of loftiness and grace, of awe and power. Whomsoever Thou willest Thou causest to draw nigh unto the Most Great Ocean, and on whomsoever Thou desirest Thou conferrest the honor of recognizing Thy Most Ancient Name. Of all who are in heaven and on earth, none can withstand the operation of Thy sovereign Will. From all eternity Thou didst rule the entire creation, and Thou wilt continue for evermore to exercise Thy dominion over all created things. There is none other God but Thee, the Almighty, The Most Exalted, the All-Powerful, the All-Wise.

Illumine, O Lord, the faces of Thy servants, that they may behold Thee; and cleanse their hearts that they may turn unto the court of Thy heavenly favors, and recognize Him Who is the Manifestation of Thy

Self and the Dayspring of Thine Essence. Verily, Thou art the Lord of all worlds. There is no God but Thee, the Unconstrained, the All-Subduing.

—Bahá'u'lláh

* * *

Glorified art Thou, O Lord my God! I yield Thee thanks for having enabled me to recognize the Manifestation of Thyself, and for having severed me from Thine enemies, and laid bare before mine eyes their misdeeds and wicked works in Thy days, and for having rid me of all attachment to them, and caused me to turn wholly towards Thy grace and bountiful favors. I give Thee thanks, also, for having sent down upon me from the clouds of Thy will that which hath so sanctified me from the hints of the infidels and the allusions of the misbelievers that I have fixed my heart firmly on Thee, and fled from such as have denied the light of Thy countenance. Again I thank Thee for having empowered me to be steadfast in Thy love, and to speak forth Thy praise and to extol Thy virtues, and for having given me to drink of the cup of Thy mercy that hath surpassed all things visible and invisible.

Thou art the Almighty, the Most Exalted, the All-Glorious, the All-Loving.

—Bahá'u'lláh

* * *

My God, my Adored One, my King, my Desire! What tongue can voice my thanks to Thee? I was heedless, Thou didst awaken me. I had turned back from Thee, Thou didst graciously aid me to turn towards Thee. I was as one dead, Thou didst quicken me with the water of life. I was withered, Thou didst revive me with the heavenly stream of Thine utterance which hath flowed forth from the Pen of the All-Merciful.

O Divine Providence! All existence is begotten by Thy bounty; deprive it not of the waters of Thy generosity, neither do Thou withhold it from the ocean of Thy mercy. I beseech Thee to aid and assist me at all times and under all conditions, and seek from the heaven of Thy grace Thine ancient favor. Thou art, in truth, the Lord of bounty, and the Sovereign of the kingdom of eternity.

—Bahá'u'lláh

* * *

Praise and Gratitude

Praised be Thou, O Lord my God! I bear witness that from eternity Thou wert exalted in Thy transcendent majesty and might, and wilt to eternity abide in Thy surpassing power and glory. None in the kingdoms of earth and heaven can frustrate Thy purpose; none throughout the realms of revelation and of creation can prevail against Thee. At Thy command Thou doest what Thou willest, and by the power of Thy sovereignty Thou rulest as Thou pleasest.

I implore Thee, O Thou Who causest the dawn to appear, by Thy Lamp which Thou didst light with the fire of Thy love before all that are in heaven and on earth, and whose flame Thou feedest with the fuel of Thy wisdom in the kingdom of Thy creation, to make me to be of those who have soared in Thine atmosphere, and surrendered their will to Thy decree.

I am all wretchedness, O my Lord, and Thou art the Most Powerful, the Almighty. Have pity upon me by Thy grace and bountiful favour, and graciously aid me to serve Thee and them that are dear to Thee. Potent art Thou to do as Thou willest. No God is there but Thee, the God of strength, of glory and wisdom.

—Bahá'u'lláh

* * *

Praise be to Thee, O Lord my God, for guiding me unto the horizon of Thy Revelation and for causing me to be mentioned by Thy Name. I beseech Thee, by the spreading rays of the Daystar of Thy providence and by the billowing waves of the Ocean of Thy mercy, to grant that my speech may bear a trace of the influence of Thine own exalted Word, attracting thereby the realities of all created things. Powerful art Thou to do what Thou willest through Thy wondrous and incomparable Utterance.

—Bahá'u'lláh

PROTECTION

Lauded be Thy name, O Lord my God! I entreat Thee by Thy Name through which the Hour hath struck, and the Resurrection came to pass, and fear and trembling seized all that are in heaven and all that are on earth, to rain down, out of the heaven of Thy mercy and the clouds of Thy tender compassion, what will gladden the hearts of Thy servants, who have turned towards Thee and helped Thy Cause.

Keep safe Thy servants and Thy handmaidens, O my Lord, from the darts of idle fancy and vain imaginings, and give them from the hands of Thy grace a draught of the soft-flowing waters of Thy knowledge.

Thou, truly, art the Almighty, the Most Exalted, the Ever-Forgiving, the Most Generous.

—Bahá'u'lláh

Lauded be Thy name, O Thou in Whose hands is the kingdom of all names, and in the grasp of Whose might are all that are in heaven and all that are on earth! I entreat Thee, by Him Who is Thy Most Effulgent Name Whom Thou hast made a target for the darts of Thy decree in Thy path, O Thou the King of eternity, to rend asunder the veils that have shut off Thy creatures from the horizon of Thy glory, that haply they may turn their faces in the direction of Thy mercy, and draw nigh unto the Day-Spring of Thy loving-kindness.

Leave not Thy servants to themselves, O my Lord! Draw them through the influence of Thine utterances unto the Dawning-Place of Thine inspiration, and to the Fountain of Thy Revelation, and to the Treasury of Thy wisdom. Thou art He to Whose strength and power all things have testified, Whose Purpose nothing whatsoever of all that hath been created in Thy heaven and on Thy earth hath been able to frustrate.

Render, then, victorious, O my God, Thy servants who have set their faces towards Thee, and directed their steps to the seat of Thy grace. Send down, then, upon them what will keep them safe from the danger of turning to any one but Thee, and from fixing their eyes upon aught else except Thyself.

Potent art Thou to do what Thou willest, and to rule as Thou pleasest. There is no God but Thee, the God of glory and wisdom.

—Bahá'u'lláh

* * *

Praised be Thou, O Lord my God! This is Thy servant who hath quaffed from the hands of Thy grace the wine of Thy tender mercy, and tasted of the savor of Thy love in Thy days. I beseech Thee, by the embodiments of Thy names whom no grief can hinder from rejoicing in Thy love or from gazing on Thy face, and whom all the hosts of the heedless are powerless to cause to turn aside from the path of Thy pleasure, to supply him with the good things Thou dost possess, and to raise him up to such heights that he will regard the world even as a shadow that vanisheth swifter than the twinkling of an eye.

Keep him safe also, O my God, by the power of Thine immeasurable majesty, from all that Thou abhorrest. Thou art, verily, his Lord and the Lord of all worlds.

—Bahá'u'lláh

* * *

O my Lord! Thou knowest that the people are encircled with pain and calamities and are environed with hardships and trouble. Every trial doth attack man and every dire adversity doth assail him like unto the assault of a serpent. There is no shelter and asylum for him except under the wing of Thy protection, preservation, guard and custody.

O Thou the Merciful One! O my Lord! Make Thy protection my armor, Thy preservation my shield, humbleness before the door of Thy oneness my guard, and Thy custody and defense my fortress and my abode. Preserve me from the suggestions of self and desire, and guard me from every sickness, trial, difficulty and ordeal.

Verily, Thou art the Protector, the Guardian, the Preserver, the Sufficer, and verily, Thou art the Merciful of the Most Merciful.

—'Abdu'l-Bahá

Protection

O Thou divine providence, pitiful are we, grant us Thy succor; homeless wanderers, give us Thy shelter; scattered, do Thou unite us; astray, gather us to Thy fold; bereft, do Thou bestow upon us a share and portion; athirst, lead us to the well-spring of Life; frail, strengthen us that we may arise to help Thy Cause and offer ourselves as a living sacrifice in the pathway of guidance.

—'Abdu'l-Bahá

* * *

O God, my God! Shield Thy trusted servants from the evils of self and passion, protect them with the watchful eye of Thy loving-kindness from all rancor, hate and envy, shelter them in the impregnable stronghold of Thy care and, safe from the darts of doubtfulness, make them the manifestations of Thy glorious signs, illumine their faces with the effulgent rays shed from the Dayspring of Thy divine unity, gladden their hearts with the verses revealed from Thy holy kingdom, strengthen their loins by Thine all-swaying power that cometh from Thy realm of glory. Thou art the All-Bountiful, the Protector, the Almighty, the Gracious.

—'Abdu'l-Bahá

SPIRITUAL ASSEMBLY

O Thou Lord of the Kingdom! Though our bodies be gathered here together, yet our spellbound hearts are carried away by Thy love, and yet are we transported by the rays of Thy resplendent face. Weak though we be, we await the revelations of Thy might and power. Poor though we be, with neither goods nor means, still take we riches from the treasures of Thy Kingdom. Drops though we be, still do we draw out from Thy ocean deeps. Motes though we be, still do we gleam in the glory of Thy splendid Sun.

O Thou our Provider! Send down Thine aid, that each one gathered here may become a lighted candle, each one a center of attraction, each one a summoner to Thy heavenly realms, till at last we make this nether world the mirror image of Thy Paradise.

—'Abdu'l-Bahá

Spiritual Assembly

O God! O God! From the unseen kingdom of Thy oneness behold us assembled in this spiritual meeting, believing in Thee, confident in Thy signs, firm in Thy Covenant and Testament, attracted to Thee, set aglow with the fire of Thy love and sincere in Thy Cause. We are servants in Thy vineyard, spreaders of Thy religion, devoted worshipers of Thy countenance, humble towards Thy loved ones, submissive before Thy door, and imploring Thee to confirm us in serving Thy chosen ones, to support us with Thine unseen hosts, to strengthen our loins in Thy servitude and to make us submissive and adoring subjects communing with Thee.

O our Lord! We are weak, and Thou art the Mighty, the Powerful. We are lifeless, and Thou art the great life-giving Spirit. We are needy, and Thou art the Sustainer, the Powerful.

O our Lord! Turn our faces unto Thy merciful countenance, feed us from Thy heavenly table with Thine abundant grace, assist us with the hosts of Thy supreme angels and confirm us through the holy ones of the Kingdom of Abhá.

Remembrance of God

Verily, Thou art the Generous, the Merciful. Thou art the Possessor of great bounty, and, verily, Thou art the Clement and the Gracious.

—'Abdu'l-Bahá

* * *

O God, my God! We are servants of Thine that have turned with devotion to Thy Holy Face, that have detached ourselves from all besides Thee in this glorious Day. We have gathered in this Spiritual Assembly, united in our views and thoughts, with our purposes harmonized to exalt Thy Word amidst mankind. O Lord, our God! Make us the signs of Thy Divine Guidance, the Standards of Thine exalted Faith amongst men, servants to Thy mighty Covenant, O Thou our Lord Most High, manifestations of Thy Divine Unity in Thine Abhá Kingdom, and resplendent stars shining upon all regions. Lord! Aid us to become seas surging with the billows of Thy wondrous Grace, streams flowing from Thine all-glorious Heights, goodly fruits upon the Tree of Thy heavenly Cause, trees waving through the breezes of Thy Bounty in Thy celestial Vineyard. O God! Make our souls dependent upon the Verses of Thy Divine Unity, our hearts cheered with the outpourings of Thy Grace, that we may unite even as the waves of one sea and become merged together as the rays of Thine effulgent Light; that our thoughts, our views, our feelings may become as one reality, manifesting the spirit of union throughout the world. Thou art the Gracious, the Bountiful, the Bestower, the Almighty, the Merciful, the Compassionate.

—'Abdu'l-Bahá

***

SPIRITUAL QUALITIES

Create in me a pure heart, O my God, and renew a tranquil conscience within me, O my Hope! Through the spirit of power confirm Thou me in Thy Cause, O my Best-Beloved, and by the light of Thy glory reveal unto me Thy path, O Thou the Goal of my desire! Through the power of Thy transcendent might lift me up unto the heaven of Thy holiness, O Source of my being, and by the breezes of Thine eternity gladden me, O Thou Who art my God! Let Thine everlasting melodies breathe tranquillity on me, O my Companion, and let the riches of Thine ancient countenance deliver me from all except Thee, O my Master, and let the tidings of the revelation of Thine incorruptible Essence bring me joy, O Thou Who art the most manifest of the manifest and the most hidden of the hidden!

—Bahá'u'lláh

Spiritual Qualities

O my Lord! Make Thy beauty to be my food, and Thy presence my drink, and Thy pleasure my hope, and praise of Thee my action, and remembrance of Thee my companion, and the power of Thy sovereignty my succorer, and Thy habitation my home, and my dwelling-place the seat Thou hast sanctified from the limitations imposed upon them who are shut out as by a veil from Thee.

Thou art, verily, the Almighty, the All-Glorious, the Most Powerful.

—Bahá'u'lláh

* * *

O my God, the God of bounty and mercy! Thou art that King by Whose commanding word the whole creation hath been called into being; and Thou art that All-Bountiful One the doings of Whose servants have never hindered Him from showing forth His grace, nor have they frustrated the revelations of His bounty.

Suffer this servant, I beseech Thee, to attain unto that which is the cause of his salvation in every world of Thy worlds. Thou art, verily, the Almighty, the Most Powerful, the All-Knowing, the All-Wise.

—Bahá'u'lláh

Suffer me, O my God, to draw nigh unto Thee, and to abide within the precincts of Thy court, for remoteness from Thee hath well-nigh consumed me. Cause me to rest under the shadow of the wings of Thy grace, for the flame of my separation from Thee hath melted my heart within me. Draw me nearer unto the river that is life indeed, for my soul burneth with thirst in its ceaseless search after Thee. My sighs, O my God, proclaim the bitterness of mine anguish, and the tears I shed attest my love for Thee.

I beseech Thee, by the praise wherewith Thou praisest Thyself and the glory wherewith Thou glorifiest Thine own Essence, to grant that we may be numbered among them that have recognized Thee and acknowledged Thy sovereignty in Thy days. Help us then to quaff, O my God, from the fingers of mercy the living waters of Thy loving-kindness, that we may utterly forget all else except Thee, and be occupied only with Thy Self. Powerful art Thou to do what Thou willest. No God is there beside Thee, the Mighty, the Help in Peril, the Self-Subsisting.

Spiritual Qualities

Glorified be Thy name, O Thou Who art the King of all Kings!

—Bahá'u'lláh

* * *

From the sweet-scented streams of Thine eternity give me to drink, O my God, and of the fruits of the tree of Thy being enable me to taste, O my Hope! From the crystal springs of Thy love suffer me to quaff, O my Glory, and beneath the shadow of Thine everlasting providence let me abide, O my Light! Within the meadows of Thy nearness, before Thy presence, make me able to roam, O my Beloved, and at the right hand of the throne of Thy mercy, seat me, O my Desire! From the fragrant breezes of Thy joy let a breath pass over me, O my Goal, and into the heights of the paradise of Thy reality let me gain admission, O my Adored One! To the melodies of the dove of Thy oneness suffer me to hearken, O Resplendent One, and through the spirit of Thy power and Thy might quicken me, O my Provider! In the spirit of Thy love keep me steadfast, O my Succorer, and in the path of Thy good pleasure set firm my steps, O my Maker! Within the garden of Thine immortality, before

Thy countenance, let me abide for ever, O Thou Who art merciful unto me, and upon the seat of Thy glory stablish me, O Thou Who art my Possessor! To the heaven of Thy loving-kindness lift me up, O my Quickener, and unto the Daystar of Thy guidance lead me, O Thou my Attractor! Before the revelations of Thine invisible spirit summon me to be present, O Thou Who art my Origin and my Highest Wish, and unto the essence of the fragrance of Thy beauty, which Thou wilt manifest, cause me to return, O Thou Who art my God!

Potent art Thou to do what pleaseth Thee. Thou art, verily, the Most Exalted, the All-Glorious, the All-Highest.

—Bahá'u'lláh

* * *

I beseech Thee, O my God, by all the transcendent glory of Thy Name, to clothe Thy loved ones in the robe of justice and to illumine their beings with the light of trustworthiness. Thou art the One that hath power to do as He pleaseth and Who holdeth within His grasp the reins of all things, visible and invisible.

—Bahá'u'lláh

Spiritual Qualities

O my Lord! O my Lord! This is a lamp lighted by the fire of Thy love and ablaze with the flame which is ignited in the tree of Thy mercy. O my Lord! Increase his enkindlement, heat and flame, with the fire which is kindled in the Sinai of Thy Manifestation. Verily, Thou art the Confirmer, the Assister, the Powerful, the Generous, the Loving.

—'Abdu'l-Bahá

* * *

O my God! O my God! This, Thy servant, hath advanced towards Thee, is passionately wandering in the desert of Thy love, walking in the path of Thy service, anticipating Thy favors, hoping for Thy bounty, relying upon Thy kingdom, and intoxicated by the wine of Thy gift. O my God! Increase the fervor of his affection for Thee, the constancy of his praise of Thee, and the ardor of his love for Thee.

Verily, Thou art the Most Generous, the Lord of grace abounding. There is no other God but Thee, the Forgiving, the Merciful.

—'Abdu'l-Bahá

Remembrance of God

O Lord! We are weak; strengthen us. O God! We are ignorant; make us knowing. O Lord! We are poor; make us wealthy. O God! We are dead; quicken us, O Lord! We are humiliation itself; glorify us in Thy kingdom. If Thou dost assist us, O Lord, we shall become as scintillating stars. If Thou dost not assist us, we shall become lower than the earth. O Lord! Strengthen us. O God! Confer victory upon us. O God! Enable us to conquer self and overcome desire. O Lord! Deliver us from the bondage of the material world. O Lord! Quicken us through the breath of the Holy Spirit in order that we may arise to serve Thee, engage in worshipping Thee, and exert ourselves in Thy kingdom with the utmost sincerity. O Lord! Thou art Powerful! O God, Thou art Forgiving! O Lord, Thou art Compassionate!

—'Abdu'l-Bahá

* * *

He is God!
O Thou kind Lord! Illumine the hearts with the light of Thy most great guidance. Revive the souls through Thy most joyful glad-tidings. Illumine the eyes by granting them to behold Thy

lights. Make the ears attentive by causing them to hear Thy call. Enable us to enter the Kingdom of Thy holiness and quicken us with the breaths of the Holy Spirit. Give us everlasting life and grant us heavenly perfections. O Lord! Make our lives to be a ransom for Thy sake and bestow upon us a new spirit. Confer upon us heavenly power and bestow upon us everlasting joy. Confirm us in service to the world of humanity. Make us instruments of concord, binding together the hearts. O Lord! Awaken us from our slumber and grant us wisdom and understanding, that we may unravel the secrets of Thy Book and discover the mysteries that lie hid in Thy Words. Thou art the Almighty. Thou art the Giver. Thou art the Ever-Loving.

—'Abdu'l-Bahá

* * *

STEADFASTNESS

Glorified be Thy Name, O Lord my God! I beseech Thee by Thy power that hath encompassed all created things, and by Thy sovereignty that hath transcended the entire creation, and by Thy Word which was hidden in Thy wisdom and whereby Thou didst create Thy heaven and Thy earth, both to enable us to be steadfast in our love for Thee and in our obedience to Thy pleasure, and to fix our gaze upon Thy face, and celebrate Thy glory. Empower us, then, O my God, to spread abroad Thy signs among Thy creatures, and to guard Thy Faith in Thy realm. Thou hast ever existed independently of the mention of any of Thy creatures, and wilt remain as Thou hast been for ever and ever.

In Thee I have placed my whole confidence, unto Thee I have turned my face, to the cord of Thy loving providence I have clung, and towards the shadow of Thy mercy I have hastened. Cast me not as one disappointed out of Thy door,

Steadfastness

O my God, and withhold not from me Thy grace, for Thee alone do I seek. No God is there beside Thee, the Ever-Forgiving, the Most Bountiful.

Praise be to Thee, O Thou Who art the Beloved of them that have known Thee!

—Bahá'u'lláh

* * *

O Thou Whose nearness is my wish, Whose presence is my hope, Whose remembrance is my desire, Whose court of glory is my goal, Whose abode is my aim, Whose name is my healing, Whose love is the radiance of my heart, Whose service is my highest aspiration! I beseech Thee by Thy Name, through which Thou hast enabled them that have recognized Thee to soar to the sublimest heights of the knowledge of Thee and empowered such as devoutly worship Thee to ascend into the precincts of the court of Thy holy favors, to aid me to turn my face towards Thy face, to fix mine eyes upon Thee, and to speak of Thy glory.

I am the one, O my Lord, who hath forgotten all else but Thee, and turned towards the Dayspring of Thy grace, who hath forsaken all save Thyself in the hope of drawing nigh unto Thy court. Behold

me, then, with mine eyes lifted up towards the
Seat that shineth with the splendors of the light
of Thy Face. Send down, then, upon me, O my
Beloved, that which will enable me to be steadfast
in Thy Cause, so that the doubts of the infidels
may not hinder me from turning towards Thee.

Thou art, verily, the God of Power, the Help in
Peril, the All-Glorious, the Almighty.

—Bahá'u'lláh

* * *

O God, my God! I have turned in repentance
unto Thee, and verily Thou art the Pardoner,
the Compassionate.

O God, my God! I have returned to Thee, and
verily Thou art the Ever-Forgiving, the Gracious.

O God, my God! I have clung to the cord of Thy
bounty, and with Thee is the storehouse of all that
is in heaven and earth.

O God, my God! I have hastened toward Thee,
and verily Thou art the Forgiver, the Lord of grace
abounding.

O God, my God! I thirst for the celestial wine
of Thy grace, and verily Thou art the Giver, the
Bountiful, the Gracious, the Almighty.

Steadfastness

O God, my God! I testify that Thou hast revealed Thy Cause, fulfilled Thy promise and sent down from the heaven of Thy grace that which hath drawn unto Thee the hearts of Thy favored ones. Well is it with him that hath held fast unto Thy firm cord and clung to the hem of Thy resplendent robe!

I ask Thee, O Lord of all being and King of the seen and unseen, by Thy power, Thy majesty and Thy sovereignty, to grant that my name may be recorded by Thy pen of glory among Thy devoted ones, them whom the scrolls of the sinful hindered not from turning to the light of Thy countenance, O prayer-hearing, prayer-answering God!

—Bahá'u'lláh

* * *

Praised and glorified art Thou, O God! Grant that the day of attaining Thy holy presence may be fast approaching. Cheer our hearts through the potency of Thy love and good-pleasure, and bestow upon us steadfastness that we may willingly submit to Thy Will and Thy Decree. Verily, Thy knowledge embraceth all the things

Thou hast created or wilt create, and Thy celestial might transcendeth whatsoever Thou hast called or wilt call into being. There is none to be worshiped but Thee, there is none to be desired except Thee, there is none to be adored besides Thee and there is naught to be loved save Thy good-pleasure.

Verily, Thou art the supreme Ruler, the Sovereign Truth, the Help in Peril, the Self-Subsisting.

\—The Báb

* * *

O compassionate God! Thanks be to Thee for Thou hast awakened and made me conscious. Thou hast given me a seeing eye and favored me with a hearing ear, hast led me to Thy kingdom and guided me to Thy path. Thou hast shown me the right way and caused me to enter the ark of deliverance. O God! Keep me steadfast and make me firm and staunch. Protect me from violent tests, and preserve and shelter me in the strongly fortified fortress of Thy Covenant and Testament. Thou art the Powerful. Thou art the Seeing. Thou art the Hearing.

Steadfastness

O Thou the Compassionate God. Bestow upon me a heart which, like unto glass, may be illumined with the light of Thy love, and confer upon me thoughts which may change this world into a rose garden through the outpourings of heavenly grace.

Thou art the Compassionate, the Merciful. Thou art the Great Beneficent God.

—'Abdu'l-Bahá

* * *

He is God!
O peerless Lord! Praised be Thou for having kindled that light in the glass of the Concourse on high, for having guided that bird of faithfulness to the nest of the Abhá Kingdom. Thou hast joined that precious river to the mighty sea, Thou hast returned that spreading of light to the Sun of Truth. Thou hast welcomed that captive of remoteness into the den of reunion, and led him who longed to look upon Thee to Thy presence in Thy bright place of lights.

Thou art the Lord of tender love, Thou art the last goal of the yearning heart, Thou art the dearest wish of the martyr's soul.

—'Abdu'l-Bahá

TEACHING

O my Lord and my Master! O my Desired One and my Best Beloved! O Thou who art the Beloved of all that are in the heavens and on the earth! I beseech Thee to grant, from the ocean of Thy bounty and the day-star of Thy heavenly grace, that I may be cursed, reviled and denounced a myriad times for the sake of Thy love, that these ears of mine may but once be blessed by hearing Thy sweet words: "Verily thou art of the people of Bahá".

—Bahá'u'lláh

* * *

Magnified be Thy name, O my God, for that Thou hast manifested the Day which is the King of Days, the Day which Thou didst announce unto Thy chosen Ones and Thy Prophets in Thy most excellent Tablets, the Day whereon Thou didst shed the splendor of the glory of all Thy names upon all created things. Great is his blessedness whosoever hath set himself towards Thee, and entered Thy presence, and caught the accents of Thy voice.

I beseech Thee, O my Lord, by the name of Him round Whom circleth in adoration the kingdom of Thy names, that Thou wilt graciously assist them that are dear to Thee to glorify Thy word among Thy servants, and to shed abroad Thy praise amidst Thy creatures, so that the ecstasies of Thy revelation may fill the souls of all the dwellers of Thine earth.

Since Thou hast guided them, O my Lord, unto the living waters of Thy grace, grant, by Thy bounty, that they may not be kept back from Thee; and since Thou hast summoned them to the habitation of Thy throne, drive them not out from Thy presence, through Thy loving-kindness. Send down upon them what shall wholly detach them from aught else except Thee, and make them able to soar in the atmosphere of Thy nearness, in such wise that neither the ascendancy of the oppressor nor the suggestions of them that have disbelieved in Thy most august and most mighty Self shall be capable of keeping them back from Thee.

—Bahá'u'lláh

Remembrance of God

O Thou incomparable God! O Thou Lord of the Kingdom! These souls are Thy heavenly army. Assist them and, with the cohorts of the Supreme Concourse, make them victorious, so that each one of them may become like unto a regiment and conquer these countries through the love of God and the illumination of divine teachings.

O God! Be Thou their supporter and their helper, and in the wilderness, the mountain, the valley, the forests, the prairies and the seas, be Thou their confidant—so that they may cry out through the power of the Kingdom and the breath of the Holy Spirit.

Verily, Thou art the Powerful, the Mighty and the Omnipotent, and Thou art the Wise, the Hearing and the Seeing.

—'Abdu'l-Bahá

* * *

O God, my God! Aid Thou Thy trusted servants to have loving and tender hearts. Help them to spread, amongst all the nations of the earth, the light of guidance that cometh from the Company on high. Verily, Thou art the Strong, the Powerful, the Mighty, the All-Subduing, the Ever-Giving. Verily, Thou art the Generous, the Gentle, the Tender, the Most Bountiful.

—'Abdu'l-Bahá

* * *

O God! O God! This is a broken-winged bird and his flight is very slow—assist him so that he may fly toward the apex of prosperity and salvation, wing his way with the utmost joy and happiness throughout the illimitable space, raise his melody in Thy Supreme Name in all the regions, exhilarate the ears with this call, and brighten the eyes by beholding the signs of guidance.

O Lord! I am single, alone and lowly. For me there is no support save Thee, no helper except Thee and no sustainer beside Thee. Confirm me in Thy service, assist me with the cohorts of Thy angels, make me victorious in the promotion of Thy Word and suffer me to speak out Thy wisdom amongst Thy creatures. Verily, Thou art the helper of the weak and the defender of the little ones, and verily Thou art the Powerful, the Mighty and the Unconstrained.

—'Abdu'l-Bahá

O my God, aid Thou Thy servant to raise up the Word, and to refute what is vain and false, to establish the truth, to spread the sacred verses abroad, reveal the splendors, and make the morning's light to dawn in the hearts of the righteous.

Thou art, verily, the Generous, the Forgiving.

—'Abdu'l-Bahá

* * *

O my God, O my God! Verily this plant hath yielded its fruit and standeth upright upon its stalk. Verily it hath astounded the farmers and perturbed the envious. O God, water it with showers from the cloud of Thy favors and cause it to yield great harvests heaped up like unto mighty hills in Thy land. Enlighten the hearts with a ray shining forth from Thy kingdom of Oneness, illumine the eyes by beholding the signs of Thy grace, and gratify the ears by hearing the melodies of the birds of Thy confirmations singing in Thy heavenly gardens, so that these souls may become like thirsty fish swimming in the pools of Thy guidance and like tawny lions roaming in the forests of Thy bounty. Verily Thou art the Generous, the Merciful, the Glorious and the Bestower.

—'Abdu'l-Bahá

Teaching

Thou knowest, O God, and art my witness that I have no desire in my heart save to attain Thy good pleasure, to be confirmed in servitude unto Thee, to consecrate myself in Thy service, to labor in Thy great vineyard and to sacrifice all in Thy path. Thou art the All-Knowing and the All-Seeing. I have no wish save to turn my steps, in my love for Thee, towards the mountains and the deserts to loudly proclaim the advent of Thy Kingdom, and to raise Thy call amidst all men. O God! Open Thou the way for this helpless one, grant Thou the remedy to this ailing one and bestow Thy healing upon this afflicted one. With burning heart and tearful eyes I supplicate Thee at Thy Threshold.

O God! I am prepared to endure any ordeal in Thy path and desire with all my heart and soul to meet any hardship.

O God! Protect me from tests. Thou knowest full well that I have turned away from all things and freed myself of all thoughts. I have no occupation save mention of Thee and no aspiration save serving Thee.

—'Abdu'l-Bahá

* * *

TESTS AND DIFFICULTIES

O Thou Whose tests are a healing medicine to such as are nigh unto Thee, Whose sword is the ardent desire of all them that love Thee, Whose dart is the dearest wish of those hearts that yearn after Thee, Whose decree is the sole hope of them that have recognized Thy truth! I implore Thee, by Thy divine sweetness and by the splendors of the glory of Thy face, to send down upon us from Thy retreats on high that which will enable us to draw nigh unto Thee. Set, then, our feet firm, O my God, in Thy Cause, and enlighten our hearts with the effulgence of Thy knowledge, and illumine our breasts with the brightness of Thy names.

—Bahá'u'lláh

* * *

Glorified art Thou, O Lord my God! Every man of insight confesseth Thy sovereignty and Thy dominion, and every discerning eye perceiveth the greatness of Thy majesty and the compelling power of Thy might. The winds of tests are powerless to hold back them that enjoy near access to Thee from setting their faces towards the horizon of Thy glory, and the tempests of trials must fail to draw away and hinder such as are wholly devoted to Thy will from approaching Thy court.

Methinks, the lamp of Thy love is burning in their hearts, and the light of Thy tenderness is lit within their breasts. Adversities are incapable of estranging them from Thy Cause, and the vicissitudes of fortune can never cause them to stray from Thy pleasure.

I beseech Thee, O my God, by them and by the sighs which their hearts utter in their separation from Thee, to keep them safe from the mischief of Thine adversaries, and to nourish their souls with what Thou hast ordained for Thy loved ones on whom shall come no fear and who shall not be put to grief.

—Bahá'u'lláh

* * *

Is there any Remover of difficulties save God? Say: Praised be God! He is God! All are His servants, and all abide by His bidding!

—The Báb

Remembrance of God

Say: God sufficeth all things above all things, and nothing in the heavens or in the earth but God sufficeth. Verily, He is in Himself the Knower, the Sustainer, the Omnipotent.

—The Báb

* * *

I adjure Thee by Thy might, O my God! Let no harm beset me in times of tests, and in moments of heedlessness guide my steps aright through Thine inspiration. Thou art God, potent art Thou to do what Thou desirest. No one can withstand Thy Will or thwart Thy Purpose.

—The Báb

* * *

O Lord! Thou art the Remover of every anguish and the Dispeller of every affliction. Thou art He Who banisheth every sorrow and setteth free every slave, the Redeemer of every soul. O Lord! Grant deliverance through Thy mercy, and reckon me among such servants of Thine as have gained salvation.

—The Báb

* * *

Tests and Difficulties

O Lord, my God and my Haven in my distress! My Shield and my Shelter in my woes! My Asylum and Refuge in time of need and in my loneliness my Companion! In my anguish my Solace, and in my solitude a loving Friend! The Remover of the pangs of my sorrows and the Pardoner of my sins!

Wholly unto Thee do I turn, fervently imploring Thee with all my heart, my mind and my tongue, to shield me from all that runs counter to Thy will in this, the cycle of Thy divine unity, and to cleanse me of all defilement that will hinder me from seeking, stainless and unsullied, the shade of the tree of Thy grace.

Have mercy, O Lord, on the feeble, make whole the sick, and quench the burning thirst.

Gladden the bosom wherein the fire of Thy love doth smolder, and set it aglow with the flame of Thy celestial love and spirit.

Robe the tabernacles of divine unity with the vesture of holiness, and set upon my head the crown of Thy favor.

Illumine my face with the radiance of the orb of Thy bounty, and graciously aid me in ministering at Thy holy threshold.

Remembrance of God

Make my heart overflow with love for Thy creatures and grant that I may become the sign of Thy mercy, the token of Thy grace, the promoter of concord amongst Thy loved ones, devoted unto Thee, uttering Thy commemoration and forgetful of self but ever mindful of what is Thine.

O God, my God! Stay not from me the gentle gales of Thy pardon and grace, and deprive me not of the wellsprings of Thine aid and favor.

Neath the shade of Thy protecting wings let me nestle, and cast upon me the glance of Thine all-protecting eye.

Loose my tongue to laud Thy name amidst Thy people, that my voice may be raised in great assemblies and from my lips may stream the flood of Thy praise.

Thou art, in all truth, the Gracious, the Glorified, the Mighty, the Omnipotent.

—'Abdu'l-Bahá

* * *

TRIUMPH OF THE CAUSE

Lauded be Thy name, O Lord my God! Darkness hath fallen upon every land, and the forces of mischief have encompassed all the nations. Through them, however, I perceive the splendors of Thy wisdom, and discern the brightness of the light of Thy providence.

They that are shut out as by a veil from Thee have imagined that they have the power to put out Thy light, and to quench Thy fire, and to still the winds of Thy grace. Nay, and to this Thy might beareth me witness! Had not every tribulation been made the bearer of Thy wisdom, and every ordeal the vehicle of Thy providence, no one would have dared oppose us, though the powers of earth and heaven were to be leagued against us. Were I to unravel the wondrous mysteries of Thy wisdom which are laid bare before me, the reins of Thine enemies would be cleft asunder.

Remembrance of God

Glorified be Thou, then, O my God! I beseech Thee by Thy Most Great Name to assemble them that love Thee around the Law that streameth from the good pleasure of Thy will, and to send down upon them what will assure their hearts.

Potent art Thou to do what pleaseth Thee. Thou art, verily, the Help in Peril, the Self-Subsisting.

—Bahá'u'lláh

* * *

O Lord! Enable all the peoples of the earth to gain admittance into the Paradise of Thy Faith, so that no created being may remain beyond the bounds of Thy good-pleasure.

From time immemorial Thou hast been potent to do what pleaseth Thee and transcendent above whatsoever Thou desirest.

—The Báb

* * *

O Lord! Render victorious Thy forbearing servants in Thy days by granting them a befitting victory, inasmuch as they have sought martyrdom in Thy path. Send down upon them that which will bring comfort to their minds, will rejoice their inner beings, will impart assurance to their hearts and tranquillity to their bodies and will enable their souls to ascend to the presence of God, the Most Exalted, and to attain the supreme Paradise and such retreats of glory as Thou hast destined for men of true knowledge and virtue. Verily, Thou knowest all things, while we are but Thy servants, Thy thralls, Thy bondsmen and Thy poor ones. No Lord but Thee do we invoke, O God our Lord, nor do we implore blessings or grace from anyone but Thee, O Thou Who art the God of mercy unto this world and the next. We are but the embodiments of poverty, of nothingness, of helplessness and of perdition, while Thy whole Being betokeneth wealth, independence, glory, majesty and boundless grace.

Turn our recompense, O Lord, into that which well beseemeth Thee of the good of this world and of the next, and of the manifold bounties which extend from on high down to the earth below.

Verily, Thou art our Lord and the Lord of all things. Into Thy hands do we surrender ourselves, yearning for the things that pertain unto Thee.

—The Báb

He is God!

O Lord, my God, my Well-Beloved! These are servants of Thine that have heard Thy Voice, given ear to Thy Word and hearkened to Thy Call. They have believed in Thee, witnessed Thy wonders, acknowledged Thy proof and testified to Thine evidence. They have walked in Thy ways, followed Thy guidance, discovered Thy mysteries, comprehended the secrets of Thy Book, the verses of Thy Scrolls and the tidings of Thy Epistles and Tablets. They have clung to the hem of Thy garment and held fast unto the robe of Thy light and grandeur. Their footsteps have been strengthened in Thy Covenant and their hearts made firm in Thy Testament. Lord! Do Thou kindle in their hearts the flame of Thy divine attraction and grant that the bird of love and understanding may sing within their hearts. Grant that they may be even as potent signs, resplendent standards, and perfect as Thy Word. Exalt by them Thy Cause, unfurl Thy banners and publish far and wide Thy wonders. Make by them Thy Word triumphant, and strengthen the loins of Thy loved ones. Unloose their tongues to laud Thy Name, and inspire them to do Thy holy will and pleasure. Illumine their faces in Thy Kingdom of holiness, and perfect their joy by aiding them to arise for the triumph of Thy Cause.

Lord! Feeble are we, strengthen us to diffuse the fragrances of Thy Holiness; poor, enrich us from the treasures of Thy Divine Unity; naked, clothe us with the robe of Thy bounty; sinful, forgive us our sins by Thy grace, Thy favor and Thy pardon. Thou art, verily, the Aider, the Helper, the Gracious, the Mighty, the Powerful.

The glory of glories rest upon them that are fast and firm.

—'Abdu'l-Bahá

***

TRUST IN GOD

O my God, O my Lord, O my Master ! I beg Thee to forgive me for seeking any pleasure save Thy love, or any comfort except Thy nearness, or any delight besides Thy good-pleasure, or any existence other than communion with Thee.

—The Báb

***

God is sufficient unto me. He verily is the All-Sufficing. In Him let the trusting trust.

—Bahá'u'lláh

***

UNITY

O my God! O my God! Unite the hearts of Thy servants, and reveal to them Thy great purpose. May they follow Thy commandments and abide in Thy law. Help them, O God, in their endeavor, and grant them strength to serve Thee. O God! Leave them not to themselves, but guide their steps by the light of Thy knowledge, and cheer their hearts by Thy love. Verily, Thou art their Helper and their Lord.

—Bahá'u'lláh

* * *

God grant that the light of unity may envelop the whole earth, and that the seal, "the Kingdom is God's", may be stamped upon the brow of all its peoples.

—Bahá'u'lláh

* * *

Remembrance of God

Glory be to Thee, O God, for Thy manifestation of love to mankind! O Thou Who art our Life and Light, guide Thy servants in Thy way, and make us rich in Thee and free from all save Thee.

O God, teach us Thy Oneness and give us a realization of Thy Unity, that we may see no one save Thee. Thou art the Merciful and the Giver of bounty!

O God, create in the hearts of Thy beloved the fire of Thy love, that it may consume the thought of everything save Thee.

Reveal to us, O God, Thine exalted eternity—that Thou hast ever been and wilt ever be, and that there is no God save Thee. Verily, in Thee will we find comfort and strength.

—Bahá'u'lláh

* * *

O Thou Who art the Lord of Lords! I testify that Thou art the Lord of all creation, and the Educator of all beings, visible and invisible. I bear witness that Thy power hath encompassed the entire universe, and that the hosts of the earth can never dismay Thee, nor can the dominion of all peoples and nations deter Thee from executing Thy purpose. I confess that Thou hast no desire except the regeneration of the whole world, and the establishment of the unity of its people, and the salvation of all them that dwell therein.

—Bahá'u'lláh

* * *

O my God! O my God! Verily, I invoke Thee and supplicate before Thy threshold, asking Thee that all Thy mercies may descend upon these souls. Specialize them for Thy favor and Thy truth.

O Lord! Unite and bind together the hearts, join in accord all the souls, and exhilarate the spirits through the signs of Thy sanctity and oneness. O Lord! Make these faces radiant through the light of Thy oneness. Strengthen the loins of Thy servants in the service of Thy kingdom.

O Lord, Thou possessor of infinite mercy! O Lord of forgiveness and pardon! Forgive our sins, pardon our shortcomings, and cause us to turn to the kingdom of Thy clemency, invoking the kingdom of might and power, humble at Thy shrine and submissive before the glory of Thine evidences.

O Lord God! Make us as waves of the sea, as flowers of the garden, united, agreed through the bounties of Thy love. O Lord! Dilate the breasts through the signs of Thy oneness, and make all mankind as stars shining from the same height of glory, as perfect fruits growing upon Thy tree of life.

Verily, Thou art the Almighty, the Self-Subsistent, the Giver, the Forgiving, the Pardoner, the Omniscient, the One Creator.

—'Abdu'l-Bahá

***

YOUTH

O Lord! Make this youth radiant, and confer Thy bounty upon this poor creature. Bestow upon him knowledge, grant him added strength at the break of every morn and guard him within the shelter of Thy protection so that he may be freed from error, may devote himself to the service of Thy Cause, may guide the wayward, lead the hapless, free the captives and awaken the heedless, that all may be blessed with Thy remembrance and praise. Thou art the Mighty and the Powerful.

—'Abdu'l-Bahá

* * *

O Thou kind Lord! From the horizon of detachment Thou hast manifested souls that, even as the shining moon, shed radiance upon the realm of heart and soul, rid themselves from the attributes of the world of existence and hastened forth unto the kingdom of immortality. With a drop from the ocean of Thy loving-kindness Thou didst oft-times moisten the gardens of their hearts until they gained incomparable freshness and beauty. The holy fragrance of Thy divine unity was diffused far and wide, shedding its sweet savors over the entire world, causing the regions of the earth to be redolent with perfume.

Raise up then, O spirit of Purity, souls who, like those sanctified beings, will become free and pure, will adorn the world of being with a new raiment and a wondrous robe, will seek no one else but Thee, tread no path except the path of Thy good pleasure and will speak of naught but the mysteries of Thy Cause.

O Thou kind Lord! Grant that this youth may attain unto that which is the highest aspiration of the holy ones. Endow him with the wings of Thy strengthening grace – wings of detachment and divine aid – that he may soar thereby into the atmosphere of Thy tender mercy, be able to partake of Thy celestial bestowals, may become a sign of divine guidance and a standard of the Concourse on high. Thou art the Potent, the Powerful, the Seeing, the Hearing.

—'Abdu'l-Bahá

PRAYERS

FOR
SPECIAL OCCASIONS
AND
HOLY WRITINGS

OBLIGATORY PRAYERS

"The daily obligatory prayers are three in number.... The believer is entirely free to choose any one of these three prayers, but is under the obligation of reciting one of them, and in accordance with any specific directions with which they may be accompanied."

—from a letter written on behalf of Shoghi Effendi

SHORT OBLIGATORY PRAYER
TO BE RECITED ONCE IN
TWENTY-FOUR HOURS, AT NOON

I bear witness, O my God, that Thou hast created me to know Thee and to worship Thee. I testify, at this moment, to my powerlessness and to Thy might, to my poverty and to Thy wealth.

There is none other God but Thee, the Help in Peril, the Self-Subsisting.

—Bahá'u'lláh

MEDIUM OBLIGATORY PRAYER

TO BE RECITED DAILY, IN THE MORNING, AT NOON, AND IN THE EVENING

Whoso wisheth to pray, let him wash his hands, and while he washeth, let him say:

Strengthen my hand, O my God, that it may take hold of Thy Book with such steadfastness that the hosts of the world shall have no power over it. Guard it, then, from meddling with whatsoever doth not belong unto it. Thou art, verily, the Almighty, the Most Powerful.

And while washing his face, let him say:

I have turned my face unto Thee, O my Lord! Illumine it with the light of Thy countenance. Protect it, then, from turning to anyone but Thee.

Then let him stand up, and facing the Qiblih (Point of Adoration, i.e. Bahjí, Akká), let him say:

God testifieth that there is none other God but Him. His are the kingdoms of Revelation and of creation. He, in truth, hath manifested Him Who is the Dayspring of Revelation, Who conversed on Sinai, through Whom the Supreme Horizon hath been made to shine, and the Lote-Tree beyond which there is no passing hath spoken, and through Whom the call hath been proclaimed unto all who are in heaven and on earth: "Lo, the All-Possessing is come. Earth and heaven, glory and dominion are God's, the Lord of all men, and the Possessor of the Throne on high and of earth below!"

Let him, then, bend down, with hands resting on the knees, and say:

Exalted art Thou above my praise and the praise of anyone beside me, above my description and the description of all who are in heaven and all who are on earth!

Then, standing with open hands, palms upward toward the face, let him say:

Disappoint not, O my God, him that hath, with beseeching fingers, clung to the hem of Thy mercy and Thy grace, O Thou Who of those who show mercy art the Most Merciful!

Let him, then, be seated and say:

I bear witness to Thy unity and Thy oneness, and that Thou art God, and that there is none other God beside Thee. Thou hast, verily, revealed Thy Cause, fulfilled Thy Covenant, and opened wide the door of Thy grace to all that dwell in heaven and on earth. Blessing and peace, salutation and glory, rest upon Thy loved ones, whom the changes and chances of the world have not deterred from turning unto Thee, and who have given their all, in the hope of obtaining that which is with Thee. Thou art, in truth, the Ever-Forgiving, the All-Bountiful.

(If anyone choose to recite instead of the long verse these words: "God testifieth that there is none other God but Him, the Help in Peril, the Self-Subsisting," it would be sufficient. And likewise, it would suffice were he, while seated,

to choose to recite these words: "I bear witness to Thy unity and Thy oneness, and that Thou art God, and that there is none other God beside Thee.")

—Bahá'u'lláh

***

"...as to the obligatory prayer (to be said three times a day): Each one must say his prayer alone by himself, and this is not conditional on a private place; that is, both at home and in the worshiping-place, which is a gathering place, it is allowable for one to say his prayer; but each person must say his prayer by himself (i.e., not in company with others who might recite the same words and continue the same postures together at the same time). But if they chant supplications (communes, etc.) together (and in company), in a good and effective voice, that is very good..."

—'Abdu'l-Bahá
Tablets of 'Abdu'l-Bahá, p. 464

LONG OBLIGATORY PRAYER

TO BE RECITED ONCE IN TWENTY-FOUR HOURS

Whoso wisheth to recite this prayer, let him stand up and turn unto God, and, as he standeth in his place, let him gaze to the right and to the left, as if awaiting the mercy of his Lord, the Most Merciful, the Compassionate. Then let him say:

O Thou Who art the Lord of all names and the Maker of the heavens! I beseech Thee by them Who are the Daysprings of Thine invisible Essence, the Most Exalted, the All-Glorious, to make of my prayer a fire that will burn away the veils which have shut me out from Thy beauty, and a light that will lead me unto the ocean of Thy Presence.

Let him then raise his hands in supplication toward God—blessed and exalted be He—and say:

Long Obligatory Prayer

O Thou the Desire of the world and the Beloved of the nations! Thou seest me turning toward Thee, and rid of all attachment to anyone save Thee, and clinging to Thy cord, through whose movement the whole creation hath been stirred up. I am Thy servant, O my Lord, and the son of Thy servant. Behold me standing ready to do Thy will and Thy desire, and wishing naught else except Thy good pleasure. I implore Thee by the Ocean of Thy mercy and the Daystar of Thy grace to do with Thy servant as Thou willest and pleasest. By Thy might which is far above all mention and praise! Whatsoever is revealed by Thee is the desire of my heart and the beloved of my soul. O God, my God! Look not upon my hopes and my doings, nay rather look upon Thy will that hath encompassed the heavens and the earth. By Thy Most Great Name, O Thou Lord of all nations! I have desired only what Thou didst desire, and love only what Thou dost love.

Let him then kneel, and bowing his forehead to the ground, let him say:

Exalted art Thou above the description of anyone save Thyself, and the comprehension of aught else except Thee.

Let him then stand and say:

Make my prayer, O my Lord, a fountain of living waters whereby I may live as long as Thy sovereignty endureth, and may make mention of Thee in every world of Thy worlds.

Let him again raise his hands in supplication, and say:

O Thou in separation from Whom hearts and souls have melted, and by the fire of Whose love the whole world hath been set aflame! I implore Thee by Thy Name through which Thou hast subdued the whole creation, not to withhold from me that which is with Thee, O Thou Who rulest over all men! Thou seest, O my Lord, this stranger hastening to his most exalted home beneath the canopy of Thy majesty and within the precincts of Thy mercy; and this transgressor seeking the ocean of Thy forgiveness; and this lowly one the court of Thy glory; and this poor creature the orient of Thy wealth. Thine is the authority to command whatsoever Thou willest.

I bear witness that Thou art to be praised in Thy doings, and to be obeyed in Thy behests, and to remain unconstrained in Thy bidding.

Let him then raise his hands, and repeat three times the Greatest Name.* Let him then bend down with hands resting on the knees before God—blessed and exalted be He—and say:

Thou seest, O my God, how my spirit hath been stirred up within my limbs and members, in its longing to worship Thee, and in its yearning to remember Thee and extol Thee; how it testifieth to that whereunto the Tongue of Thy Commandment hath testified in the kingdom of Thine utterance and the heaven of Thy knowledge. I love, in this state, O my Lord, to beg of Thee all that is with Thee, that I may demonstrate my poverty, and magnify Thy bounty and Thy riches, and may declare my powerlessness, and manifest Thy power and Thy might.

Let him then stand and raise his hands twice in supplication, and say:

_____
* Alláh-u-Abhá

Remembrance of God

There is no God but Thee, the Almighty, the All-Bountiful. There is no God but Thee, the Ordainer, both in the beginning and in the end. O God, my God! Thy forgiveness hath emboldened me, and Thy mercy hath strengthened me, and Thy call hath awakened me, and Thy grace hath raised me up and led me unto Thee. Who, otherwise, am I that I should dare to stand at the gate of the city of Thy nearness, or set my face toward the lights that are shining from the heaven of Thy will? Thou seest, O my Lord, this wretched creature knocking at the door of Thy grace, and this evanescent soul seeking the river of everlasting life from the hands of Thy bounty. Thine is the command at all times, O Thou Who art the Lord of all names; and mine is resignation and willing submission to Thy will, O Creator of the heavens!

Let him then raise his hands thrice, and say:

Greater is God than every great one!

Let him then kneel and, bowing his forehead to the ground, say:

Long Obligatory Prayer

Too high art Thou for the praise of those who are nigh unto Thee to ascend unto the heaven of Thy nearness, or for the birds of the hearts of them who are devoted to Thee to attain to the door of Thy gate. I testify that Thou hast been sanctified above all attributes and holy above all names. No God is there but Thee, the Most Exalted, the All-Glorious.

Let him then seat himself and say:

I testify unto that whereunto have testified all created things, and the Concourse on high, and the inmates of the all-highest Paradise, and beyond them the Tongue of Grandeur itself from the all-glorious Horizon, that Thou art God, that there is no God but Thee, and that He Who hath been manifested is the Hidden Mystery, the Treasured Symbol, through Whom the letters B and E (Be) have been joined and knit together. I testify that it is He Whose name hath been set down by the Pen of the Most High, and Who hath been mentioned in the Books of God, the Lord of the Throne on high and of earth below.

Let him then stand erect and say:

Remembrance of God

O Lord of all being and Possessor of all things visible and invisible! Thou dost perceive my tears and the sighs I utter, and hearest my groaning, and my wailing, and the lamentation of my heart. By Thy might! My trespasses have kept me back from drawing nigh unto Thee; and my sins have held me far from the court of Thy holiness. Thy love, O my Lord, hath enriched me, and separation from Thee hath destroyed me, and remoteness from Thee hath consumed me. I entreat Thee by Thy footsteps in this wilderness, and by the words "Here am I. Here am I" which Thy chosen Ones have uttered in this immensity, and by the breaths of Thy Revelation, and the gentle winds of the Dawn of Thy Manifestation, to ordain that I may gaze on Thy beauty and observe whatsoever is in Thy Book.

Let him then repeat the Greatest Name thrice, and bend down with hands resting on the knees, and say:

Praise be to Thee, O my God, that Thou hast aided me to remember Thee and to praise Thee, and hast made known unto me Him Who is the Dayspring of Thy signs, and hast caused me to bow down before Thy Lordship, and humble myself before Thy Godhead, and to acknowledge that which hath been uttered by the Tongue of Thy grandeur.

Let him then rise and say:

O God, my God! My back is bowed by the burden of my sins, and my heedlessness hath destroyed me. Whenever I ponder my evil doings and Thy benevolence, my heart melteth within me, and my blood boileth in my veins. By Thy Beauty, O Thou the Desire of the world! I blush to lift up my face to Thee, and my longing hands are ashamed to stretch forth toward the heaven of Thy bounty. Thou seest, O my God, how my tears prevent me from remembering Thee and from extolling Thy virtues, O Thou the Lord of the Throne on high and of earth below! I implore Thee by the signs of Thy Kingdom and the mysteries of Thy Dominion to do with Thy loved ones as becometh Thy bounty, O Lord of all being, and is worthy of Thy grace, O King of the seen and the unseen!

Remembrance of God

Let him then repeat the Greatest Name thrice, and kneel with his forehead to the ground, and say:

Praise be unto Thee, O our God, that Thou hast sent down unto us that which draweth us nigh unto Thee, and supplieth us with every good thing sent down by Thee in Thy Books and Thy Scriptures. Protect us, we beseech Thee, O my Lord, from the hosts of idle fancies and vain imaginations. Thou, in truth, art the Mighty, the All-Knowing.

Let him then raise his head, and seat himself, and say:

I testify, O my God, to that whereunto Thy chosen Ones have testified, and acknowledge that which the inmates of the all-highest Paradise and those who have circled round Thy mighty Throne have acknowledged. The kingdoms of earth and heaven are Thine, O Lord of the worlds!

—Bahá'u'lláh

***

TABLET OF AḤMAD

He is the King, the All-Knowing, the Wise!
Lo, the Nightingale of Paradise singeth upon the twigs of the Tree of Eternity, with holy and sweet melodies, proclaiming to the sincere ones the glad tidings of the nearness of God, calling the believers in the Divine Unity to the court of the Presence of the Generous One, informing the severed ones of the message which hath been revealed by God, the King, the Glorious, the Peerless, guiding the lovers to the seat of sanctity and to this resplendent Beauty.

Verily this is that Most Great Beauty, foretold in the Books of the Messengers, through Whom truth shall be distinguished from error and the wisdom of every command shall be tested. Verily He is the Tree of Life that bringeth forth the fruits of God, the Exalted, the Powerful, the Great.

O Aḥmad! Bear thou witness that verily He is God and there is no God but Him, the King, the Protector, the Incomparable, the Omnipotent. And that the One Whom He hath sent forth by the name of 'Alí* was the true One from God, to Whose commands we are all conforming.

Say: O people be obedient to the ordinances of God, which have been enjoined in the Bayán by the Glorious, the Wise One. Verily He is the King of the Messengers and His Book is the Mother Book did ye but know.

Thus doth the Nightingale utter His call unto you from this prison. He hath but to deliver this clear message. Whosoever desireth, let him turn aside from this counsel and whosoever desireth let him choose the path to his Lord.

O people, if ye deny these verses, by what proof have ye believed in God? Produce it, O assemblage of false ones.

Nay, by the One in Whose hand is my soul, they are not, and never shall be able to do this, even should they combine to assist one another.

O Aḥmad! Forget not My bounties while I am absent. Remember My days during thy days, and

---

* The Báb

My distress and banishment in this remote prison. And be thou so steadfast in My love that thy heart shall not waver, even if the swords of the enemies rain blows upon thee and all the heavens and the earth arise against thee.

Be thou as a flame of fire to My enemies and a river of life eternal to My loved ones, and be not of those who doubt.

And if thou art overtaken by affliction in My path, or degradation for My sake, be not thou troubled thereby.

Rely upon God, thy God and the Lord of thy fathers. For the people are wandering in the paths of delusion, bereft of discernment to see God with their own eyes, or hear His Melody with their own ears. Thus have We found them, as thou also dost witness.

Thus have their superstitions become veils between them and their own hearts and kept them from the path of God, the Exalted, the Great.

Be thou assured in thyself that verily, he who turns away from this Beauty hath also turned away from the Messengers of the past and showeth pride towards God from all eternity to all eternity.

Remembrance of God

Learn well this Tablet, O Aḥmad. Chant it during thy days and withhold not thyself therefrom. For verily, God hath ordained for the one who chanteth it, the reward of a hundred martyrs and a service in both worlds. These favors have We bestowed upon thee as a bounty on Our part and a mercy from Our presence, that thou mayest be of those who are grateful.

By God! Should one who is in affliction or grief read this Tablet with absolute sincerity, God will dispel his sadness, solve his difficulties and remove his afflictions.

Verily, He is the Merciful, the Compassionate. Praise be to God, the Lord of all the worlds.

—Bahá'u'lláh

FIRE TABLET

(This Tablet is revealed by Bahá'u'lláh entitled "Qad-Ihtaraqa'l-Mukhlisún")

In the Name of God, the Most Ancient, the Most Great.

Indeed the hearts of the sincere are consumed in the fire of separation:

> Where is the gleaming of the light of Thy Countenance, O Beloved of the worlds?

Those who are near unto Thee have been abandoned in the darkness of desolation:

> Where is the shining of the morn of Thy reunion, O Desire of the worlds?

The bodies of Thy chosen ones lie quivering on distant sands:

> Where is the ocean of Thy presence, O Enchanter of the worlds?

Remembrance of God

Longing hands are uplifted to the heaven of Thy grace and generosity:

> Where are the rains of Thy bestowal, O Answerer of the worlds?

The infidels have arisen in tyranny on every hand:

> Where is the compelling power of Thine ordaining pen, O Conqueror of the worlds?

The barking of dogs is loud on every side:

> Where is the lion of the forest of Thy might, O Chastiser of the worlds?

Coldness hath gripped all mankind:

> Where is the warmth of Thy love, O Fire of the worlds?

Calamity hath reached its height:

> Where are the signs of Thy succor, O Salvation of the worlds?

Darkness hath enveloped most of the peoples:

> Where is the brightness of Thy splendour, O Radiance of the worlds?

Fire Tablet

The necks of men are stretched out in malice:

> Where are the swords of Thy vengeance,
> O Destroyer of the worlds?

Abasement hath reached its lowest depth:

> Where are the emblems of Thy glory,
> O Glory of the worlds?

Sorrows have afflicted the Revealer of Thy Name, the All-Merciful:

> Where is the joy of the Dayspring of Thy Revelation, O Delight of the worlds?

Anguish hath befallen all the peoples of the earth:

> Where are the ensigns of Thy gladness,
> O Joy of the worlds?

Thou seest the Dawning Place of Thy signs veiled by evil suggestions:

> Where are the fingers of Thy might, O Power of the worlds?

Sore thirst hath overcome all men:

> Where is the river of Thy bounty, O Mercy of the worlds?

Remembrance of God

Greed hath made captive all mankind:

> Where are the embodiments of detachment, O Lord of the worlds?

Thou seest this Wronged One lonely in exile:

> Where are the hosts of the heaven of Thy Command, O Sovereign of the worlds?

I have been forsaken in a foreign land:

> Where are the emblems of Thy faithfulness, O Trust of the worlds?

The agonies of death have laid hold on all men:

> Where is the surging of Thine ocean of eternal life, O Life of the worlds?

The whisperings of Satan have been breathed to every creature:

> Where is the meteor of Thy fire, O Light of the worlds?

The drunkenness of passion hath perverted most of mankind:

> Where are the daysprings of purity, O Desire of the worlds?

Fire Tablet

Thou seest this Wronged One veiled in tyranny among the Syrians:

> Where is the radiance of Thy dawning light,
> O Light of the worlds?

Thou seest Me forbidden to speak forth:

> Then from where will spring Thy melodies,
> O Nightingale of the worlds?

Most of the people are enwrapped in fancy and idle imaginings:

> Where are the exponents of Thy certitude,
> O Assurance of the worlds?

Bahá is drowning in a sea of tribulation:

> Where is the Ark of Thy salvation, O Saviour
> of the worlds?

Thou seest the Dayspring of Thine utterance in the darkness of creation:

> Where is the sun of the heaven of Thy grace,
> O Lightgiver of the worlds?

The lamps of truth and purity, of loyalty and honour, have been put out:

Where are the signs of Thine avenging wrath, O Mover of the worlds?

Canst Thou see any who have championed Thy Self, or who ponder on what hath befallen Him in the pathway of Thy love?

Now doth My pen halt, O Beloved of the worlds.

The branches of the Divine Lote-Tree lie broken by the onrushing gales of destiny:

Where are the banners of Thy succor, O Champion of the worlds?

This Face is hidden in the dust of slander:

Where are the breezes of Thy compassion, O Mercy of the worlds?

The robe of sanctity is sullied by the people of deceit:

Where is the vesture of Thy holiness, O Adorner of the worlds?

The sea of grace is stilled for what the hands of men have wrought:

Where are the waves of Thy bounty, O Desire of the worlds?

Fire Tablet

The door leading to the Divine Presence is locked through the tyranny of Thy foes:

> Where is the key of Thy bestowal, O Unlocker of the worlds?

The leaves are yellowed by the poisoning winds of sedition:

> Where is the downpour of the clouds of Thy bounty, O Giver of the worlds?

The universe is darkened with the dust of sin:

> Where are the breezes of Thy forgiveness, O Forgiver of the worlds?

This Youth is lonely in a desolate land:

> Where is the rain of Thy heavenly grace, O Bestower of the worlds?

O Supreme Pen, We have heard Thy most sweet call in the eternal realm:

> Give Thou ear unto what the Tongue of Grandeur uttereth, O Wronged One of the worlds!

Remembrance of God

Were it not for the cold,

> How would the heat of Thy words prevail,
> O Expounder of the worlds?

Were it not for calamity,

> How would the sun of Thy patience shine,
> O Light of the worlds?

Lament not because of the wicked.

> Thou wert created to bear and endure,
> O Patience of the worlds.

How sweet was Thy dawning on the horizon of the Covenant among the stirrers of sedition, and Thy yearning after God, O Love of the worlds.

By Thee the banner of independence was planted on the highest peaks, and the sea of bounty surged, O Rapture of the worlds.

By Thine aloneness the Sun of Oneness shone,

> and by Thy banishment the land of Unity was adorned. Be patient, O Thou Exile of the worlds.

Fire Tablet

We have made abasement the garment of glory,
and affliction the adornment of Thy temple,
O Pride of the worlds.

Thou seest the hearts are filled with hate,
and to overlook is Thine, O Thou Concealer
of the sins of the worlds.

When the swords flash, go forward!
When the shafts fly, press onward! O Thou
Sacrifice of the worlds.

Dost Thou wail, or shall I wail? Rather shall
I weep at the fewness of Thy champions,
O Thou Who hast caused the wailing of the
worlds.

Verily, I have heard Thy Call, O All-Glorious
Beloved; and now is the face of Bahá flaming with
the heat of tribulation and with the fire of Thy
shining word, and He hath risen up in faithfulness
at the place of sacrifice, looking toward Thy
pleasure, O Ordainer of the worlds.

Remembrance of God

O 'Alí-Akbar, thank thy Lord for this Tablet whence thou canst breathe the fragrances of My meekness, and know what hath beset Us in the path of God, the Adored of all the worlds.

Should all the servants read and ponder this, there shall be kindled in their veins a fire that shall set aflame the worlds.

—Bahá'u'lláh

* * *

TABLET OF VISITATION

The praise which hath dawned from Thy most august Self, and the glory which hath shone forth from Thy most effulgent Beauty, rest upon Thee, O Thou Who art the Manifestation of Grandeur, and the King of Eternity, and the Lord of all who are in heaven and on earth! I testify that through Thee the sovereignty of God and His dominion, and the majesty of God and His grandeur, were revealed, and the Daystars of ancient splendor have shed their radiance in the heaven of Thine irrevocable decree, and the Beauty of the Unseen hath shone forth above the horizon of creation. I testify, moreover, that with but a movement of Thy Pen Thine injunction "Be Thou" hath been enforced, and God's hidden Secret hath been divulged, and all created things have been called into being, and all the Revelations have been sent down.

I bear witness, moreover, that through Thy beauty the beauty of the Adored One hath been unveiled, and through Thy face the face of the Desired One hath shone forth, and that through a word from Thee Thou hast decided between all created things, causing them who are devoted to Thee to ascend unto the summit of glory, and the infidels to fall into the lowest abyss.

I bear witness that he who hath known Thee hath known God, and he who hath attained unto Thy presence hath attained unto the presence of God. Great, therefore, is the blessedness of him who hath believed in Thee, and in Thy signs, and hath humbled himself before Thy sovereignty, and hath been honored with meeting Thee, and hath attained the good pleasure of Thy will, and circled around Thee, and stood before Thy throne. Woe betide him that hath transgressed against Thee, and hath denied Thee, and repudiated Thy signs, and gainsaid Thy sovereignty, and risen up against Thee, and waxed proud before Thy face, and hath disputed Thy testimonies, and fled from Thy rule and Thy dominion, and been numbered with the infidels whose names have been inscribed by the fingers of Thy behest upon Thy holy Tablets.

Waft, then, unto me, O my God and my Beloved, from the right hand of Thy mercy and Thy loving-kindness, the holy breaths of Thy favors, that they may draw me away from myself and from the world unto the courts of Thy nearness and Thy presence. Potent art Thou to do what pleaseth Thee. Thou, truly, hast been supreme over all things.

The remembrance of God and His praise, and the glory of God and His splendor, rest upon Thee, O Thou Who art His Beauty! I bear witness that the eye of creation hath never gazed upon one wronged like Thee. Thou wast immersed all the days of Thy life beneath an ocean of tribulations. At one time Thou wast in chains and fetters; at another Thou wast threatened by the sword of Thine enemies. Yet, despite all this, Thou didst enjoin upon all men to observe what had been prescribed unto Thee by Him Who is the All-Knowing, the All-Wise.

May my spirit be a sacrifice to the wrongs Thou didst suffer, and my soul be a ransom for the adversities Thou didst sustain. I beseech God, by Thee and by them whose faces have been illumined with the splendors of the light of Thy countenance, and who, for love of Thee, have observed all whereunto they were bidden, to remove the veils that have come in between Thee and Thy creatures, and to supply me with the good of this world and the world to come. Thou art, in truth, the Almighty, the Most Exalted, the All-Glorious, the Ever-Forgiving, the Most Compassionate.

Bless Thou, O Lord my God, the Divine Lote-Tree and its leaves, and its boughs, and its branches, and its stems, and its offshoots, as long as Thy most excellent titles will endure and Thy most august attributes will last. Protect it, then, from the mischief of the aggressor and the hosts of tyranny. Thou art, in truth, the Almighty, the Most Powerful. Bless Thou, also, O Lord my God, Thy servants and Thy handmaidens who have attained unto Thee. Thou, truly, art the All-Bountiful, Whose grace is infinite. No God is there save Thee, the Ever-Forgiving, the Most Generous.

—Bahá'u'lláh

PRAYER OF VISITATION OF 'ABDU'L-BAHÁ

This prayer, revealed by 'Abdu'l-Bahá, is read at His Shrine. It is also used in private prayer.

"Whoso reciteth this prayer with lowliness and fervor will bring gladness and joy to the heart of this Servant; it will be even as meeting Him face to face."

He is the All-Glorious!

O God, my God! Lowly and tearful, I raise my suppliant hands to Thee and cover my face in the dust of that Threshold of Thine, exalted above the knowledge of the learned, and the praise of all that glorify Thee. Graciously look upon Thy servant, humble and lowly at Thy door, with the glances of the eye of Thy mercy, and immerse him in the Ocean of Thine eternal grace.

Lord! He is a poor and lowly servant of Thine, enthralled and imploring Thee, captive in Thy hand, praying fervently to Thee, trusting in

Thee, in tears before Thy face, calling to Thee and beseeching Thee, saying:

O Lord, my God! Give me Thy grace to serve Thy loved ones, strengthen me in my servitude to Thee, illumine my brow with the light of adoration in Thy court of holiness, and of prayer to Thy kingdom of grandeur. Help me to be selfless at the heavenly entrance of Thy gate, and aid me to be detached from all things within Thy holy precincts. Lord! Give me to drink from the chalice of selflessness; with its robe clothe me, and in its ocean immerse me. Make me as dust in the pathway of Thy loved ones, and grant that I may offer up my soul for the earth ennobled by the footsteps of Thy chosen ones in Thy path, O Lord of Glory in the Highest.

With this prayer doth Thy servant call Thee, at dawntide and in the night-season. Fulfill his heart's desire, O Lord! Illumine his heart, gladden his bosom, kindle his light, that he may serve Thy Cause and Thy servants.

Thou art the Bestower, the Pitiful, the Most Bountiful, the Gracious, the Merciful, the Compassionate.

—'Abdu'l-Bahá

THE LONG HEALING PRAYER

He is the Healer, the Sufficer, the Helper, the All-Forgiving, the All-Merciful.

I call on Thee O Exalted One, O Faithful One, O Glorious One! Thou the Sufficing, Thou the Healing, Thou the Abiding, O Thou Abiding One!

I call on Thee O Sovereign, O Upraiser, O Judge! Thou the Sufficing, Thou the Healing, Thou the Abiding, O Thou Abiding One!

I call on Thee O Peerless One, O Eternal One, O Single One! Thou the Sufficing, Thou the Healing, Thou the Abiding, O Thou Abiding One!

I call on Thee O Most Praised One, O Holy One, O Helping One! Thou the Sufficing, Thou the Healing, Thou the Abiding, O Thou Abiding One!

I call on Thee O Omniscient, O Most Wise, O Most Great One! Thou the Sufficing, Thou the Healing, Thou the Abiding, O Thou Abiding One!

Remembrance of God

I call on Thee O Clement One, O Majestic One, O Ordaining One! Thou the Sufficing, Thou the Healing, Thou the Abiding, O Thou Abiding One!

I call on Thee O Beloved One, O Cherished One, O Enraptured One! Thou the Sufficing, Thou the Healing, Thou the Abiding, O Thou Abiding One!

I call on Thee O Mightiest One, O Sustaining One, O Potent One! Thou the Sufficing, Thou the Healing, Thou the Abiding, O Thou Abiding One!

I call on Thee O Ruling One, O Self-Subsisting, O All-Knowing One! Thou the Sufficing, Thou the Healing, Thou the Abiding, O Thou Abiding One!

I call on Thee O Spirit, O Light, O Most Manifest One! Thou the Sufficing, Thou the Healing, Thou the Abiding, O Thou Abiding One!

I call on Thee O Thou Frequented by all, O Thou Known to all, O Thou Hidden from all! Thou the Sufficing, Thou the Healing, Thou the Abiding, O Thou Abiding One!

The Long Healing Prayer

I call on Thee O Concealed One, O Triumphant One, O Bestowing One! Thou the Sufficing, Thou the Healing, Thou the Abiding, O Thou Abiding One!

I call on Thee O Almighty, O Succoring One, O Concealing One! Thou the Sufficing, Thou the Healing, Thou the Abiding, O Thou Abiding One!

I call on Thee O Fashioner, O Satisfier, O Uprooter! Thou the Sufficing, Thou the Healing, Thou the Abiding, O Thou Abiding One!

I call on Thee O Rising One, O Gathering One, O Exalting One! Thou the Sufficing, Thou the Healing, Thou the Abiding, O Thou Abiding One!

I call on Thee O Perfecting One, O Unfettered One, O Bountiful One! Thou the Sufficing, Thou the Healing, Thou the Abiding, O Thou Abiding One!

I call on Thee O Beneficent One, O Withholding One, O Creating One! Thou the Sufficing, Thou the Healing, Thou the Abiding, O Thou Abiding One!

Remembrance of God

I call on Thee O Most Sublime One, O Beauteous One, O Bounteous One! Thou the Sufficing, Thou the Healing, Thou the Abiding, O Thou Abiding One!

I call on Thee O Just One, O Gracious One, O Generous One! Thou the Sufficing, Thou the Healing, Thou the Abiding, O Thou Abiding One!

I call on Thee O All-Compelling, O Ever-Abiding, O Most Knowing One! Thou the Sufficing, Thou the Healing, Thou the Abiding, O Thou Abiding One!

I call on Thee O Magnificent One, O Ancient of Days, O Magnanimous One! Thou the Sufficing, Thou the Healing, Thou the Abiding, O Thou Abiding One!

I call on Thee O Well-guarded One, O Lord of Joy, O Desired One! Thou the Sufficing, Thou the Healing, Thou the Abiding, O Thou Abiding One!

I call on Thee O Thou Kind to all, O Thou Compassionate with all, O Most Benevolent One! Thou the Sufficing, Thou the Healing, Thou the Abiding, O Thou Abiding One!

The Long Healing Prayer

I call on Thee O Haven for all, O Shelter to all, O All-Preserving One! Thou the Sufficing, Thou the Healing, Thou the Abiding, O Thou Abiding One!

I call on Thee O Thou Succorer of all, O Thou Invoked by all, O Quickening One! Thou the Sufficing, Thou the Healing, Thou the Abiding, O Thou Abiding One!

I call on Thee O Unfolder, O Ravager, O Most Clement One! Thou the Sufficing, Thou the Healing, Thou the Abiding, O Thou Abiding One!

I call on Thee O Thou my Soul, O Thou my Beloved, O Thou my Faith! Thou the Sufficing, Thou the Healing, Thou the Abiding, O Thou Abiding One!

I call on Thee O Quencher of thirsts, O Transcendent Lord, O Most Precious One! Thou the Sufficing, Thou the Healing, Thou the Abiding, O Thou Abiding One!

I call on Thee O Greatest Remembrance, O Noblest Name, O Most Ancient Way! Thou the Sufficing, Thou the Healing, Thou the Abiding, O Thou Abiding One!

Remembrance of God

I call on Thee O Most Lauded, O Most Holy, O Sanctified One! Thou the Sufficing, Thou the Healing, Thou the Abiding, O Thou Abiding One!

I call on Thee O Unfastener, O Counselor, O Deliverer! Thou the Sufficing, Thou the Healing, Thou the Abiding, O Thou Abiding One!

I call on Thee O Friend, O Physician, O Captivating One! Thou the Sufficing, Thou the Healing, Thou the Abiding, O Thou Abiding One!

I call on Thee O Glory, O Beauty, O Bountiful One! Thou the Sufficing, Thou the Healing, Thou the Abiding, O Thou Abiding One!

I call on Thee O the Most Trusted, O the Best Lover, O Lord of the Dawn! Thou the Sufficing, Thou the Healing, Thou the Abiding, O Thou Abiding One!

I call on Thee O Enkindler, O Brightener, O Bringer of Delight! Thou the Sufficing, Thou the Healing, Thou the Abiding, O Thou Abiding One!

I call on Thee O Lord of Bounty, O Most Compassionate, O Most Merciful One! Thou the

The Long Healing Prayer

Sufficing, Thou the Healing, Thou the Abiding, O Thou Abiding One!

I call on Thee O Constant One, O Life-giving One, O Source of all Being! Thou the Sufficing, Thou the Healing, Thou the Abiding, O Thou Abiding One!

I call on Thee O Thou Who penetratest all things, O All-Seeing God, O Lord of Utterance! Thou the Sufficing, Thou the Healing, Thou the Abiding, O Thou Abiding One!

I call on Thee O Manifest yet Hidden, O Unseen yet Renowned, O Onlooker sought by all! Thou the Sufficing, Thou the Healing, Thou the Abiding, O Thou Abiding One!

I call on Thee O Thou Who slayest the Lovers, O God of Grace to the wicked!

O Sufficer, I call on Thee, O Sufficer!

O Healer, I call on Thee, O Healer!

O Abider, I call on Thee, O Abider!

Thou the Ever-Abiding, O Thou Abiding One!

Sanctified art Thou, O my God! I beseech Thee by Thy generosity, whereby the portals of Thy bounty and grace were opened wide, whereby the Temple of Thy Holiness was established upon the throne of eternity; and by Thy mercy whereby Thou didst invite all created things unto the table of Thy bounties and bestowals; and by Thy grace whereby Thou didst respond, in Thine own Self with Thy word "Yea!" on behalf of all in heaven and earth, at the hour when Thy sovereignty and Thy grandeur stood revealed, at the dawn-time when the might of Thy dominion was made manifest. And again do I beseech Thee, by these most beauteous names, by these most noble and sublime attributes, and by Thy most Exalted Remembrance, and by Thy pure and spotless Beauty, and by Thy hidden Light in the most hidden pavilion, and by Thy Name, cloaked with the garment of affliction every morn and eve, to protect the bearer of this blessed Tablet, and whoso reciteth it, and whoso cometh upon it, and whoso passeth around the house wherein it is. Heal Thou, then, by it every sick, diseased and poor one, from every tribulation and distress, from every loathsome affliction and sorrow, and guide Thou by it whosoever desireth to enter upon the paths of Thy guidance, and the ways of Thy forgiveness and grace.

Thou art verily the Powerful, the All-Sufficing, the Healing, the Protector, the Giving, the Compassionate, the All-Generous, the All-Merciful.

—Bahá'u'lláh

***

THE FAST

Praise be to Thee, O Lord my God! I beseech Thee by this Revelation whereby darkness hath been turned into light, through which the Frequented Fane hath been built, and the Written Tablet revealed, and the Outspread Roll uncovered, to send down upon me and upon them who are in my company that which will enable us to soar into the heavens of Thy transcendent glory, and will wash us from the stain of such doubts as have hindered the suspicious from entering into the tabernacle of Thy unity.

I am the one, O my Lord, who hath held fast the cord of Thy loving-kindness, and clung to the hem of Thy mercy and favors. Do Thou ordain for me and for my loved ones the good of this world and of the world to come. Supply them, then, with the Hidden Gift Thou didst ordain for the choicest among Thy creatures.

The Fast

These are, O my Lord, the days in which Thou hast bidden Thy servants to observe the Fast. Blessed is he that observeth the Fast wholly for Thy sake and with absolute detachment from all things except Thee. Assist me and assist them, O my Lord, to obey Thee and to keep Thy precepts. Thou, verily, hast power to do what Thou choosest.

There is no God but Thee, the All-Knowing, the All-Wise. All praise be to God, the Lord of all worlds.

—Bahá'u'lláh

***

O Divine Providence! As I am abstaining from bodily desires and not occupied with eating and drinking, even so purify and sanctify my heart from the love of anyone save Thyself, and shield and protect my soul from corrupt desires and satanic qualities, so that my spirit may commune with the breaths of holiness, and fast from the mention of all else besides Thee.

—'Abdu'l-Bahá

***

NAW-RÚZ

Praised be Thou, O my God, that Thou hast ordained Naw-Rúz as a festival unto those who have observed the Fast for love of Thee and abstained from all that is abhorrent unto Thee. Grant, O my Lord, that the fire of Thy love and the heat produced by the Fast enjoined by Thee may inflame them in Thy Cause, and make them to be occupied with Thy praise and with remembrance of Thee.

Since Thou hast adorned them, O my Lord, with the ornament of the Fast prescribed by Thee, do Thou adorn them also with the ornament of Thine acceptance, through Thy grace and bountiful favor. For the doings of men are all dependent upon Thy good pleasure, and are conditioned by Thy behest. Shouldst Thou regard him who hath broken the Fast as one who hath observed it, such a man would be reckoned among them who from eternity had been keeping the Fast. And shouldst Thou decree that he who hath observed the Fast hath broken it, that person would be numbered with such as have caused the Robe of Thy Revelation to be stained with dust, and been far removed from the crystal waters of this living Fountain.

Thou art He through Whom the ensign "Praiseworthy art Thou in Thy works" hath been lifted up, and the standard "Obeyed art Thou in Thy behest" hath been unfurled. Make known this Thy station, O my God, unto Thy servants, that they may be made aware that the excellence of all things is dependent upon Thy bidding and Thy word, and the virtue of every act is conditioned by Thy leave and the good pleasure of Thy will, and may recognize that the reins of men's doings are within the grasp of Thine acceptance and Thy commandment. Make this known unto them, that nothing whatsoever may shut them out from Thy Beauty, in these days whereon the Christ exclaimeth: "All dominion is Thine, O Thou the Begetter of the Spirit (Jesus)"; and Thy Friend (Muhammad) crieth out: "Glory be to Thee, O Thou the Best-Beloved, for that Thou hast uncovered

Thy Beauty, and written down for Thy chosen ones what will cause them to attain unto the seat of the revelation of Thy Most Great Name, through which all the peoples have lamented except such as have detached themselves from all else except Thee, and set themselves towards Him Who is the Revealer of Thyself and the Manifestation of Thine attributes."

He Who is Thy Branch and all Thy company, O my Lord, have broken this day their fast, after having observed it within the precincts of Thy court, and in their eagerness to please Thee. Do Thou ordain for Him, and for them, and for all such as have entered Thy presence in those days all the good Thou didst destine in Thy Book. Supply them, then, with that which will profit them, in both this life and in the life beyond.

Thou, in truth, art the All-Knowing, the All-Wise.

—Bahá'u'lláh

THE RIḌVÁN TABLET
(Excerpts)

The Divine Springtime is come, O Most Exalted Pen, for the Festival of the All-Merciful is fast approaching. Bestir thyself, and magnify, before the entire creation, the name of God, and celebrate His praise, in such wise that all created things may be regenerated and made new. Speak, and hold not Thy peace. The day star of blissfulness shineth above the horizon of Our name, the Blissful, inasmuch as the kingdom of the name of God hath been adorned with the ornament of the name of Thy Lord, the creator of the heavens. Arise before the nations of the earth, and arm thyself with the power of this Most Great Name, and be not of those who tarry...

This is the Day whereon the unseen world crieth out: "Great is thy blessedness, O earth, for thou hast been made the foot-stool of thy God, and been chosen as the seat of His mighty throne."

The realm of glory exclaimeth: "Would that my life could be sacrificed for thee, for He Who is the Beloved of the All-Merciful hath established His sovereignty upon thee, through the power of His Name that hath been promised unto all things, whether of the past or of the future." ....

The Best-Beloved is come. In His right hand is the sealed Wine of His name. Happy is the man that turneth unto Him, and drinketh his fill, and exclaimeth: "Praise be to Thee, O Revealer of the signs of God!" By the righteousness of the Almighty! Every hidden thing hath been manifested through the power of truth. All the favors of God have been sent down, as a token of His grace. The waters of everlasting life have, in their fullness, been proffered unto men. Every single cup hath been borne round by the hand of the Well-Beloved. Draw near, and tarry not, though it be for one short moment...

Rejoice with exceeding gladness, O people of Bahá, as ye call to remembrance the Day of supreme felicity, the Day whereon the Tongue of the Ancient of Days hath spoken, as He departed from His House, proceeding to the Spot from which He shed upon the whole of creation the splendors of His name, the All-Merciful. God is Our witness. Were We to reveal the hidden secrets of that Day, all they that dwell on earth and in the heavens would swoon away and die, except such as will be preserved by God, the Almighty, the All-Knowing, the All-Wise.

Such is the inebriating effect of the words of God upon Him Who is the Revealer of His undoubted proofs, that His pen can move no longer. With these words He concludeth His Tablet: "No God is there but Me, the Most Exalted, the Most Powerful, the Most Excellent, the All-Knowing.

—Bahá'u'lláh

***

MARRIAGE

The pledge of marriage, the verse to be spoken individually by the bride and the bridegroom in the presence of at least two witnesses acceptable to the Spiritual Assembly is, as stipulated in the Kitáb-i-Aqdas (The Most Holy Book):

"We will all, verily, abide by the Will of God."

He is the Bestower, the Bounteous!

Praise be to God, the Ancient, the Ever-Abiding, the Changeless, the Eternal! He Who hath testified in His Own Being that verily He is the One, the Single, the Untrammelled, the Exalted. We bear witness that verily there is no God but Him, acknowledging His oneness, confessing His singleness. He hath ever dwelt in unapproachable heights, in the summits of His loftiness, sanctified from the mention of aught save Himself, free from the description of aught but Him.

Marriage

And when He desired to manifest grace and beneficence to men, and to set the world in order, He revealed observances and created laws; among them He established the law of marriage, made it as a fortress for well-being and salvation, and enjoined it upon us in that which was sent down out of the heaven of sanctity in His Most Holy Book. He saith, great is His glory: "Marry, O people, that from you may appear he who will remember Me amongst My servants; this is one of My commandments unto you; obey it as an assistance to yourselves."

—Bahá'u'lláh

Glory be unto Thee, O my God! Verily, this Thy servant and this Thy maidservant have gathered under the shadow of Thy mercy and they are united through Thy favor and generosity. O Lord! Assist them in this Thy world and Thy kingdom and destine for them every good through Thy bounty and grace. O Lord! Confirm them in Thy servitude and assist them in Thy service. Suffer them to become the signs of Thy Name in Thy world and protect them through Thy bestowals which are inexhaustible in this world and the world to come. O Lord! They are supplicating the kingdom of Thy mercifulness and invoking the realm of Thy singleness. Verily, they are married in obedience to Thy command. Cause them to become the signs of harmony and unity until the end of time. Verily, Thou art the Omnipotent, the Omnipresent and the Almighty!

—'Abdu'l-Bahá

He is God!

O peerless Lord! In Thine almighty wisdom Thou hast enjoined marriage upon the peoples, that the generations of men may succeed one another in this contingent world, and that ever, so long as the world shall last, they may busy themselves at the Threshold of Thy oneness with servitude and worship, with salutation, adoration and praise. "I have not created spirits and men, but that they should worship me."* Wherefore, wed Thou in the heaven of Thy mercy these two birds of the nest of Thy love, and make them the means of attracting perpetual grace; that from

---

* Qur'án 51:56

the union of these two seas of love a wave of tenderness may surge and cast the pearls of pure and goodly issue on the shore of life. "He hath let loose the two seas, that they meet each other: Between them is a barrier which they overpass not. Which then of the bounties of your Lord will ye deny? From each He bringeth up greater and lesser pearls."†

O Thou kind Lord! Make Thou this marriage to bring forth coral and pearls. Thou art verily the All-Powerful, the Most Great, the Ever-Forgiving.

—'Abdu'l-Bahá

***

---

† Qur'án 55:19-22

DYNAMICS OF PRAYERS

The below five steps were suggested by the beloved Guardian Shoghi Effendi to a believer as a means of finding a solution through the use of prayer. This statement, belongs to the category of statements known as "pilgrims notes", and as such has no authority, but since it seems to be particularly helpful and clear it was felt that believers should not be deprived of it.

1st Step:
Pray and meditate about it. Use the prayers of the Manifestations as they have the greatest power. Then remain in the silence of contemplation for a few minutes.

2nd Step:
Arrive at a decision and hold this. This decision is usually born during the contemplation. It may seem almost impossible of accomplishment but if

it seems to be as answer to a prayer or a way of solving the problem, then immediately take the next step.

3rd Step:
Have determination to carry the decision through. Many fail here. The decision budding into determination, is blighted and instead becomes a wish or a vague longing. When determination is born, immediately take the next step.

4th Step:
Have faith and confidence that the power will flow through you, the right way will appear, the door will open, the right thought, the right message, the right principle, or the right book will be given to you. Have confidence and the right thing will come to your need. Then, as you rise from prayer, take at once the 5th step.

5th Step:
Act as though it had all been answered. Then act with tireless, ceaseless energy. And as you act, you, yourself, will become a magnet, which

will attract more power to your being, until you become an unobstructed channel for the Divine power to flow through you.

Many pray but do not remain for the last half of the first step. Some who meditate arrive at a decision, but fail to hold it. Few have the determination to carry the decision through, still fewer have the confidence that the right thing will come to their need. But how many remember to act as though it had all been answered? How true are these words "Greater than the prayer is the spirit in which it is uttered" and greater than the way it is uttered is the spirit in which it is carried out.

—Shoghi Effendi

* * *